Fossil Ridge Public Library District
25452 Kennedy Road
Braidwood, Illinois 60408

GAYLORD

PONTIAC

p. 6.

Sauvage de La f. 10. Nation

outaouaks.

Pipe

Sac apetun

NORTH AMERICAN INDIANS OF ACHIEVEMENT

PONTIAC
Ottawa Rebel

▽ ▽ ▽

Celia Bland

Senior Consulting Editor
W. David Baird
Howard A. White Professor of History
Pepperdine University

CHELSEA HOUSE PUBLISHERS

New York   Philadelphia

FRONTISPIECE   This drawing, completed around 1700, shows an Ottawa Indian carrying a long-stemmed pipe and tobacco pouch. The sun on the man's chest may represent a decorative breastplate; his jewelry, hairstyle, and body ornamentation are typical of the period.

ON THE COVER   An eloquent speaker and subtle strategist, Pontiac united the Great Lakes tribes in a campaign to drive the British from North America. His majestic bearing and fierce patriotism impressed even his enemies.

Chelsea House Publishers
EDITORIAL DIRECTOR   Richard Rennert
EXECUTIVE MANAGING EDITOR   Karyn Gullen Browne
COPY CHIEF   Robin James
PICTURE EDITOR   Adrian G. Allen
ART DIRECTOR   Robert Mitchell
MANUFACTURING DIRECTOR   Gerald Levine

North American Indians of Achievement
SENIOR EDITOR   Marian W. Taylor

Staff for PONTIAC
ASSISTANT EDITOR   Margaret Dornfeld
EDITORIAL ASSISTANT   Annie McDonnell
SENIOR DESIGNER   Rae Grant
PICTURE RESEARCHER   Alan Gottlieb
COVER ILLUSTRATOR   Shelley Pritchett

Printed and bound in Mexico.

First Printing

1   3   5   7   9   8   6   4   2

Library of Congress Cataloging-in-Publication Data

Bland, Celia.
Pontiac: Ottawa rebel/Celia Bland; senior consulting editor, W. David Baird.
    p. cm.—(North American Indians of achievement)
Includes bibliographical references and index.
ISBN 0-7910-1717-6
ISBN 0-7910-2043-6 (pbk)
1. Pontiac, Ottawa Chief, d. 1769—Juvenile literature. 2. Pontiac's Conspiracy, 1763–1765—Juvenile literature. 3. Ottawa Indians—Biography—Juvenile literature. [1. Pontiac, Ottawa Chief, d. 1769. 2. Ottawa Indians—Biography. 3. Indians of North America—Biography.] I. Baird, W. David. II. Title. III. Series.
E83.76.P66B53 1994   94-1688
973'.04973'092—dc20   CIP
[B]   AC

CONTENTS

On Indian Leadership
by *W. David Baird*   7

1   A Bad Bird Sings   11

2   The Most Formidable People in the World   23

3   The Rivers Will Run with Rum   35

4   "Something Not Right Is Brewing"   47

5   Besieged   59

6   "A Damn'd Drubbing"   71

7   Bushy Run and the Niagara Massacre   83

8   Neither Monument Nor Tombstone   95

    Chronology   107

    Further Reading   108

    Index   109

NORTH AMERICAN INDIANS OF ACHIEVEMENT

BLACK HAWK
Sac Rebel

JOSEPH BRANT
Mohawk Chief

BEN NIGHTHORSE CAMPBELL
Cheyenne Chief
and U.S. Senator

COCHISE
Apache Chief

CRAZY HORSE
Sioux War Chief

CHIEF GALL
Sioux War Chief

GERONIMO
Apache Warrior

HIAWATHA
Founder of the
Iroquois Confederacy

CHIEF JOSEPH
Nez Perce Leader

PETER MACDONALD
Former Chairman of
the Navajo Nation

WILMA MANKILLER
Principal Chief of the Cherokees

OSCEOLA
Seminole Rebel

QUANAH PARKER
Comanche Chief

KING PHILIP
Wampanoag Rebel

POCAHONTAS
Powhatan Peacemaker

PONTIAC
Ottawa Rebel

RED CLOUD
Sioux War Chief

WILL ROGERS
Cherokee Entertainer

SITTING BULL
Chief of the Sioux

TECUMSEH
Shawnee Rebel

JIM THORPE
Sac and Fox Athlete

SARAH WINNEMUCCA
Northern Paiute Writer and Diplomat

Other titles in preparation

ON INDIAN LEADERSHIP

by W. David Baird
Howard A. White Professor of History
Pepperdine University

Authoritative utterance is in thy mouth, perception is in thy heart, and thy tongue is the shrine of justice," the ancient Egyptians said of their king. From him, the Egyptians expected authority, discretion, and just behavior. Homer's *Iliad* suggests that the Greeks demanded somewhat different qualities from their leaders: justice and judgment, wisdom and counsel, shrewdness and cunning, valor and action. It is not surprising that different people living at different times should seek different qualities from the individuals they looked to for guidance. By and large, a people's requirements for leadership are determined by two factors: their culture and the unique circumstances of the time and place in which they live.

Before the late 15th century, when non-Indians first journeyed to what is now North America, most Indian tribes were not ruled by a single person. Instead, there were village chiefs, clan headmen, peace chiefs, war chiefs, and a host of other types of leaders, each with his or her own specific duties. These influential people not only decided political matters but also helped shape their tribe's social, cultural, and religious life. Usually, Indian leaders held their positions because they had won the respect of their peers. Indeed, if a leader's followers at any time decided that he or she was out of step with the will of the people, they felt free to look to someone else for advice and direction.

Thus, the greatest achievers in traditional Indian communities were men and women of extraordinary talent. They were not only skilled at navigating the deadly waters of tribal politics and cultural customs but also able to, directly or indirectly, make a positive and significant difference in the daily life of their followers.

7

From the beginning of their interaction with Native Americans, non-Indians failed to understand these features of Indian leadership. Early European explorers and settlers merely assumed that Indians had the same relationship with their leaders as non-Indians had with their kings and queens. European monarchs generally inherited their positions and ruled large nations however they chose, often with little regard for the desires or needs of their subjects. As a result, the settlers of Jamestown saw Pocahontas as a "princess" and Pilgrims dubbed Wampanoag leader Metacom "King Philip," envisioning them in roles very different from those in which their own people placed them.

As more and more non-Indians flocked to North America, the nature of Indian leadership gradually began to change. Influential Indians no longer had to take on the often considerable burden of pleasing only their own people; they also had to develop a strategy of dealing with the non-Indian newcomers. In a rapidly changing world, new types of Indian role models with new ideas and talents continually emerged. Some were warriors; others were peacemakers. Some held political positions within their tribes; others were writers, artists, religious prophets, or athletes. Although the demands of Indian leadership altered from generation to generation, several factors that determined which Indian people became prominent in the centuries after first contact remained the same.

Certain personal characteristics distinguished these Indians of achievement. They were intelligent, imaginative, practical, daring, shrewd, uncompromising, ruthless, and logical. They were constant in friendships, unrelenting in hatreds, affectionate with their relatives, and respectful to their God or gods. Of course, no single Native American leader embodied all these qualities, nor these qualities only. But it was these characteristics that allowed them to succeed.

The special skills and talents that certain Indians possessed also brought them to positions of importance. The life of Hiawatha, the legendary founder of the powerful Iroquois Confederacy, displays the value that oratorical ability had for many Indians in power.

The biography of Cochise, the 19th-century Apache chief, illustrates that leadership often required keen diplomatic skills not only in transactions among tribespeople but also in hardheaded negotiations with non-Indians. For others, such as Mohawk Joseph Brant and Navajo Peter MacDonald, a non-Indian education proved advantageous in their dealings with other peoples.

Sudden changes in circumstance were another crucial factor in determining who became influential in Indian communities. King Philip in the 1670s and Geronimo in the 1880s both came to power when their people were searching for someone to lead them into battle against white frontiersmen who had forced upon them a long series of indignities. Seeing the rising discontent of Indians of many tribes in the 1810s, Tecumseh and his brother, the Shawnee prophet Tenskwatawa, proclaimed a message of cultural revitalization that appealed to thousands. Other Indian achievers recognized cooperation with non-Indians as the most advantageous path during their lifetime. Sarah Winnemucca in the late 19th century bridged the gap of understanding between her people and their non-Indian neighbors through the publication of her autobiography *Life Among the Piutes*. Olympian Jim Thorpe in the early 20th century championed the assimilationist policies of the U.S. government and, with his own successes, demonstrated the accomplishments Indians could make in the non-Indian world. And Wilma Mankiller, principal chief of the Cherokees, continues to fight successfully for the rights of her people through the courts and through negotiation with federal officials.

Leadership among Native Americans, just as among all other peoples, can be understood only in the context of culture and history. But the centuries that Indians have had to cope with invasions of foreigners in their homelands have brought unique hardships and obstacles to the Native American individuals who most influenced and inspired others. Despite these challenges, there has never been a lack of Indian men and women equal to these tasks. With such strong leaders, it is no wonder that Native Americans remain such a vital part of this nation's cultural landscape.

1

A BAD BIRD SINGS

In the spring of 1763, when the ice had barely melted from the rivers and lakes of central and eastern North America, thousands of Indians set out to attend a secret council in what is now the state of Michigan. Shawnees, Delawares, and Miamis traveled from the distant Ohio Valley; Ottawas, Ojibwas, Potawatomis, and Hurons came from the shores of the Great Lakes. By April 27, 20,000 Indians were encamped in the forests along the banks of the Ecorse River, barely 10 miles from Fort Detroit.

When it was time for the council to begin, heralds moved from lodge to lodge calling the Indians together, and warriors and tribal elders assembled in a large clearing. Francis Parkman, a 19th-century historian, described the scene:

> Ojibwas, with quivers slung at their backs, and light war-clubs resting in the hollow of their arms; Ottawas, wrapped close in their gaudy blankets; Wyandots [a subtribe of the Hurons], fluttering in painted shirts, their heads adorned with feathers, and their leggings garnished with bells. All were soon seated in a wide circle upon the grass, row within row, a grave and silent assembly. . . . Pipes with ornamented stems were lighted, and passed from hand to hand.

The Ottawa war chief Pontiac raises a wampum belt before a group of Indian followers. One of Pontiac's greatest strengths was his power to persuade and inspire through oratory.

Finally, one of the Indians strode into the center of the clearing to address the assembly. He was small and compact, his legs, arms, and back decorated with colorful tattoos—inky interlocking circles and small faces that had been etched into his skin with needles. He was clothed in a simple loincloth, and his black hair was worn in a style favored by Indians of the Ottawa tribe, combed back from his forehead in a greased pompadour and cut short to give his enemies less to hold on to in battle. He wore a collar of white feathers around his neck, and a stone pierced his nose. For a moment he gazed at the assembled Indians, his dark eyes intense.

This man was Pontiac, a war chief of the Ottawas. Long before word of the secret council had spread through the forests of eastern North America, Pontiac's reputation as a brilliant warrior and inspiring speaker was well known among the tribes who lived there.

Slowly and with great emphasis, Pontiac began his eloquent speech. According to Parkman, he told the gathered Indians of a prophet of the Delaware Indians, Neolin, who had spoken in a dream with the Great Spirit, the ruler of heaven and earth. Pontiac said that the Great Spirit had told Neolin,

> I am the Maker of mankind, and because I love you, you must do my will. The land on which you live I have made for you, and not for others. Why do you suffer the white men to dwell among you? My children, you have forgotten the customs and traditions of your forefathers. . . . You have bought guns, knives, kettles, and blankets from the white men, until you can no longer do without them; and what is worse, you have drunk the poison fire-water, which turns you into fools. Fling all these things away; live as your wise forefathers lived before you. And as for these English, these dogs dressed in red who have come to rob you of your hunting-grounds and drive away the game, you must lift the hatchet against them. Wipe them from the face of the earth, and then you will win my favor back again, and once more be happy and prosperous.

As Pontiac recounted Neolin's dream, he paused repeatedly to allow tribal interpreters to translate his speech to their people. He also handed out wampum, belts of string, shells, and colored glass beads woven into distinct patterns, each representing an idea or resolution. Wampum served as records for councils and treaties. Months or even years later, the important points of Pontiac's speech could be reconstructed with the aid of these belts.

Parkman relates that Pontiac held one above his head as he urged his listeners to action. The war chief told them he had a plan to capture Fort Detroit and drive the British from the vast wilderness that is now called Michigan, Ohio, Indiana, and Illinois:

> I have sent wampum belts and messengers to our brothers the Chippewas of Saginaw, and to our brothers the Ottawas of Michilimackinac, and to those of the Thames River to join us. They will not be slow in coming, but while we wait let us strike anyway. There is no more time to lose. When the English are defeated we shall then see what there is left to do, and we shall stop up the ways hither so that they may never come again upon our lands.

According to French fur traders who witnessed the scene, the famous war chief concluded his speech with these words: "The children of your great father, the King of France, are not like the English. Never forget that they are your brethren. . . . They love the red men, and understand the true mode of worshiping [the Great Spirit]."

Pontiac's message was clear: the French were the Indians' allies, the British their enemy. Only a few years earlier, the British had gone to war against the French, recruiting Indian warriors from many tribes to aid them in their campaign. The British were victorious, but when the war was won the British ignored the Indians who had helped them. Many French traders and soldiers had married into Indian families, but British soldiers were forbidden to socialize with "savages." Indians were no

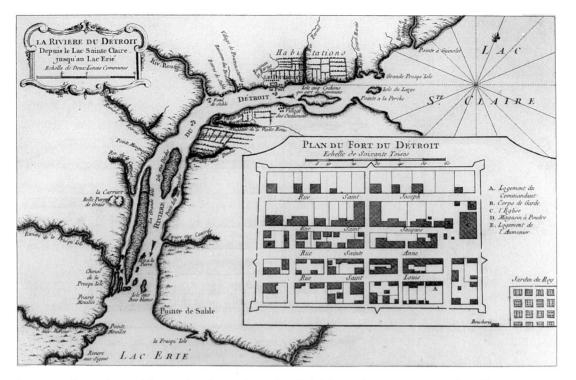

This map of the Detroit River, drawn in the 1750s, shows Fort Detroit and the settlements around it. By 1760, the fort boasted about 2,000 inhabitants.

longer allowed to visit at the forts that the British took over from the defeated French.

As if that were not enough, General Jeffrey Amherst, commander-in-chief of King George III's troops in North America, had issued orders forbidding the sale or free distribution of ammunition to the Indians, severely hampering their ability to hunt enough game to survive the winter. The sale of rum was also prohibited. In an attempt to save money, the British had stopped presenting gifts to the Indians, breaking a tradition begun by the more generous French. Now, with this secret council taking place in the Michigan forest, such short-sighted measures seemed likely to bring about a very bloody and expensive war.

Pontiac continued his oratory to the gathered tribes. Within a fortnight, he confidently told them, he would launch a surprise attack against Fort Detroit. That would be a signal to all the Indians to rise up against British garrisons in their own regions. Pontiac's scheme was met by loud whoops of approval and anticipation. The Ottawa war chief's ability to organize such a huge assembly from among many far-flung tribes proved he was a great leader, and his listeners put great faith in his plan.

The secret council ended, and the Indians returned to their distant tribes, persuaded by Pontiac's oratory and excited by the prospect of a successful war against a common enemy. Pontiac and his warriors waited patiently in the Michigan forests for the right moment to launch their attack.

By the beginning of May, Indian hunters and trappers were returning to their villages after spending the winter months deep in the wilderness. The trading posts around Fort Detroit were bustling with activity as the Indians bartered their furs for cloth, blankets, beer, and grain. A limited supply of bullets and gunpowder was available, but only at very high prices, much to the Indians' annoyance. After all, when Fort Detroit had been controlled by the French only a few years earlier, ammunition had been provided free of charge.

Alarming rumors swept through the Indian villages. It was said that once the Indians had exhausted their scant supplies of ammunition, British soldiers would strike, driving the Indians from their lands. Meanwhile, tales of the Indians' plans somehow came to the ears of British officers in Fort Detroit.

Unaware that word of his intentions had been leaked to the enemy, Pontiac proceeded according to his strategy. On May 1, with some 40 hand-picked warriors in tow, he appeared at the gates of Fort Detroit. When questioned by the sentries, Pontiac assured them that he and his men had only come to smoke the red calumet, or peace pipe, and dance the calumet dance. These rituals were an annual tradition of the Ottawa Indians, and Pontiac told the guards that they reaffirmed his tribe's loyalty to British rule.

Major Henry Gladwin, the commanding officer of Fort Detroit, reluctantly allowed the warriors to enter. He watched in silence as the Indians leaped and danced, singing of their exploits in battle. But while the dancers provided a distraction, several warriors melted into the crowd, calculating the number of soldiers in the garrison and locating the stores and houses that could be plundered for valuables.

Major Gladwin's second-in-command, Captain Donald Campbell, thanked the Indians for their performance.

No one knows for certain how the British learned of Pontiac's plan to attack Fort Detroit on May 7, 1763. According to one legend, an Indian woman named Catherine divulged the plan while delivering a pair of moccasins to Major Henry Gladwin. This 1863 painting by John M. Stanley shows Catherine approaching the officer in his quarters.

Pontiac graciously apologized for the small number of dancers, explaining that not all of the warriors had as yet come back from the winter hunt. His people would return in a few days, he said slyly, but with more warriors, and they would dance again.

When they returned to the Ottawa village, Pontiac's spies recounted what they had seen and heard. Pontiac then sent messengers to the Potawatomis, to the Ottawas at nearby L'Arbre Croche, and to the Hurons and the Ojibwas, announcing another war council to be held in the Potawatomi village, about two miles below Fort Detroit, on May 5.

The Indians gathered on the appointed day, and once again Pontiac stepped into the circle to speak. Parkman relates that the war chief told the assembly,

> It is important for us, my brothers, that we exterminate from our lands this nation which seeks only to destroy us. The English sell us goods twice as dear as the French do, and their goods do not last. . . . When I go to see the English commander and say to him that some of our comrades are dead, instead of bewailing their death, as our French brothers do, he laughs at me and at you. If I ask anything for our sick, he refuses. From all this you can well see that they are seeking our ruin. Therefore, my brothers, we must all swear their destruction and wait no longer. Nothing prevents us; they are few in numbers, and we can accomplish it.

Pontiac outlined a plan of battle and the assembled conspirators listened carefully, nodding their approval.

May 7 dawned, a warm, sunny day, and as usual Fort Detroit's gates were wide open. Throughout the morning, some 250 Ottawa men and women entered the fort in small groups, apparently to barter goods. They mixed unobtrusively with the British traders. But instead of trade goods, they had brought filed-down rifles and tomahawks, weapons they kept concealed under their multicolored blankets. That afternoon, Pontiac appeared at the fort's gate, accompanied by 60 chiefs in full war paint. They entered without interference. All was going according to plan.

Once inside the fort, however, Pontiac saw immediately that something was wrong. More than the usual number of sentries were on duty, and bayonets had been affixed to their cocked rifles. On the parade ground immediately in front of the gates, more armed soldiers stood at the ready, their guns aimed at the Indians. Even the cannons mounted on the fort's ramparts had been turned around and aimed inside the fort's walls.

Pontiac realized that his plot had been foiled; somehow, reports of the planned attack had spread to the British. Carefully concealing his disappointment, the Ottawa war chief entered the council house, followed by Major Gladwin and Captain Campbell. A solemn drum beat began to sound from the parade ground. After the traditional eating of bread and smoking of pipes, Pontiac spoke:

> We have come as is our custom to profess our friendship for the English and to smoke the pipe of peace with our good friends. Why do I see so many of your young men outside with guns? We are greatly surprised, brother, at this unusual step you have taken, to have all your soldiers under arms and that all of your young chiefs are not here for this council as they have always been before. We would be very glad to know the reason for this. Could it be that some bad bird has sung in your ear ill news of us?

Shrewdly, Major Gladwin replied that his men customarily drilled to maintain their discipline. Furthermore, he had heard that some distant Indian nation was coming to a council at the fort. Since he was unsure of their intentions, he told Pontiac, he thought it best to have his men ready.

Without saying anything more, Pontiac reached into

his blanket, and the English officers grasped their weapons in alarm. The tension in the room was palpable. Pontiac pulled out a belt of wampum, white on the top side and green on the bottom. Major Gladwin knew that when Pontiac turned the green side upward, it was a signal to his warriors to begin the attack.

Pontiac held the wampum with the white side up and spoke of six Ottawa chiefs who had died over the winter. He hoped the English would give them presents to heal the grief the Ottawas felt for their dead leaders. As he spoke, his hand rose. It seemed to the officers that he might turn the wampum belt green side up at any moment.

Gladwin gave one of his men a discreet hand signal, and word was immediately relayed to the solitary drummer outside to increase the tempo. Once again the tension in the room rose. Throughout Fort Detroit, soldiers raised their guns and aimed at the Indians on the parade ground. Pontiac froze. There was a lengthy pause. All eyes were on the white-and-green wampum belt in Pontiac's hand. The Ottawa war chief extended his hand and gave the belt to Gladwin—white side up.

Pontiac had decided that an attack that day would be futile, but when he spoke, his words held a subtle threat. "It is not fitting that we should have come to you with so few to honor you. We will go now, and in a few days we will come back with our entire nation . . . and hold a council in which we will properly express to you the friendship between the Ottawa and the English." Obviously angry, the war chief stalked from the chamber, followed by his people. The Indians filed through the gate and down to the Detroit River, where their canoes waited.

An impromptu council was held upon their return to the Ottawa village, and Pontiac was publicly rebuked for

A 19th-century painting by Frederic Remington shows Pontiac's men abandoning plans to attack Fort Detroit.

his cowardice. By refusing to give the signal to attack, his fellow leaders insisted, he had humiliated his warriors before their enemy. Pontiac remonstrated fiercely with the other chiefs. He reminded them of the preparations the British had made; clearly they had been warned of his plans. The war chief swore that he would discover the "bad bird" who had sung to the enemy, informing them of his conspiracy. And Pontiac also vowed that very soon he would launch another attack. This time he would hit his enemy where they were most vulnerable—at the British settlements that lay outside the protective walls of Fort Detroit.

2

THE MOST FORMIDABLE PEOPLE IN THE WORLD

An Ottawa warrior brandishes a bow and shield in this 1619 engraving. Probably based on verbal accounts, this stylized French illustration is the earliest known picture of an Ottawa Indian.

Pontiac was born on the north bank of the Detroit River near the present-day city of Detroit, sometime in the 1720s. According to some accounts, he was the son of an Ojibwa father and an Ottawa mother. His name—*Bwondiac* or *Obwandiyag,* as it was pronounced in his native tongue—meant "Stopping It" in the Ottawa language. In accordance with the tradition of his people, it was given to him at a naming ceremony when he was a few months old. At the same time, the infant Pontiac's ears and nose were pierced with sharpened bone. The Ottawas believed this would protect him from evil influences.

Little is known of Pontiac's early life, but it is likely that he lived with his family in a longhouse, a loaf-shaped cabin constructed of stripped saplings that had been driven into the ground. The tips of these saplings were curved together and tied, then the roof laid with fir and cedar bark. Many of these cabins were an impressive 100 to 130 feet in length and more than 20 feet wide. In most villages four or five longhouses lined a central street. Pontiac's village was probably fenced by a wall of sharpened posts driven into the ground—a defensive measure the Indians had learned from the French.

La pesche des Sauuages p. 15

passinassioneK Je decris cette pesche ailleur qui est une des choses les meruuilleuses touchand La f. 19 Pesche.

This 17th-century French drawing illustrates Great Lakes Indian fishing methods. The Indian on the left is using a long-handled net; other equipment is shown at the bottom of the picture.

As a baby, Pontiac would have been swaddled and carried in a cradleboard on his mother's back while she worked. Indian women planted their tribe's communal fields with maize, squash, peas, beans, melons, and pumpkins during the spring. This was also the season for net-fishing in the shallows of the Detroit River. During the short, hot summer, the Ottawas organized lacrosse games with each other and with Indians from other tribes. Meanwhile, if the tribe held a grudge against a neighboring village, its warriors might wage a brief campaign to resolve it. Making war against enemies was an important part of Ottawa life, but the Indians generally confined their battles to the summer months, as the region's harsh winters required them to devote their energies to survival.

The Ottawa Indians' political organization was fluid and democratic. Each village informally elected several chiefs who wielded authority for as long as their people respected them—and no longer. Some of these leaders—known to the whites as peace chiefs—would advise the tribe in civil matters; others—called war chiefs—led their people in battle. Chieftainship was not a hereditary position. If a man proved himself an excellent warrior, tactician, diplomat, and magistrate, he was elected war chief.

When Pontiac reached his teenage years, he probably followed his father on hunting trips and into battle against the tribe's enemies. Like other Indian boys, he undoubtedly participated in the village's councils, feasts, and *midewiwin*s, or religious ceremonies. Hand-to-hand combat, the torture of defeated enemies, and the negotiation of peace treaties were also necessary skills for a warrior to learn. Pontiac would have absorbed his lessons by participating and observing.

Summer was a time for courtship as well, which often took place by way of ritual dances. Ottawa women donned their fine porcelain jewelry, greased their black hair with bear oil, and painted their faces with vermilion, a brilliant red pigment. A French onlooker described one summer's revel:

> They dance to the sound of the drum and of the rattle, which is a sort of gourd with pellets of lead inside. There are four or five young men who sing, and keep time by beating the drum and the rattle, while the women dance to the rhythm and do not miss a step.

When Pontiac reached adulthood, he undoubtedly participated in these dances. It is known that he had at least two wives and two sons.

The women harvested their maize and other vegetables in the fall and set about preserving food for the coming winter. They ground corn into flour and dried squash, pumpkins, and berries in the sun. In the evenings, groups of women told stories as they shelled peas and beans by the campfires. Maple sugar was used to sweeten hominy, a dish made from ground corn formed into cakes and dribbled with bear oil. Migrating geese and ducks would fill the sky, and Ottawa hunters would shoot as many of them as they could and smoke the meat.

In October or November, Ottawa families would pack their belongings for the winter hunt. Only the very old and the sick remained behind in the village. The rest of the Indians moved south into the Ohio Valley, where they lived in tipis—cone-shaped structures made of sapling frames covered with birch bark—hunting and trapping deer, bear, buffalo, beaver, otter, fox, and raccoons.

The Ottawas had not always made their livelihood in this region. Centuries before the first Europeans came to North America, the Ottawa, Ojibwa, and Potawatomi Indians had all lived along the northeastern Atlantic coast as one tribe. As game in this region became more scarce, the Indians began moving west, toward the center of the continent. Eventually they divided into separate tribes and set up villages along the shores of the Great Lakes. When the Ottawa Indians were first encountered by French explorers in the early 1600s, they lived on small islands in Lake Huron and along the banks of Lake Nipissing, in what is now the Canadian province of Ontario. The Potawatomis and Ojibwas inhabited the forests along the shores of Lake Superior and Lake Michigan.

Soon after French traders moved into the Great Lakes region, the Ottawas began to play a central role in the fur trade. The rifle, ax, knife, jewelry, and clothing shown in this 18th-century engraving of an Ojibwa family are all European products obtained through trade.

As the Ottawas came into contact with Europeans, their way of life began to change. By the middle of the 17th century, French explorers had penetrated the Great Lakes region, and the Ottawas' neighbors, the Iroquois and the Hurons, had begun trading furs with the newcomers. In 1653, a war broke out between the Iroquois and the Hurons, disrupting the profitable fur trade. The shrewd Ottawas stepped in to take up trading where their neighbors had left off.

Displaying a fine business sense, the Ottawas bartered with the Ojibwa Indians for beaver and bear furs, then went to the French and exchanged the furs for steel axes,

knives, rifles, and blankets. Such items were new to
Indian culture and much sought after. The Ottawas
trekked long distances to other Indian villages deep in
the interior of North America, in the areas now known
as Michigan and Illinois. There they exchanged European
goods for more furs, reaping a healthy profit. In this way,
the Ottawas became a wealthy and powerful tribe.
According to historian Howard Peckham, within 30 years
they were supplying a third of all the beaver pelts bought
by the French in North America.

Unfortunately, as the whites began to encroach on the
Indians' hunting grounds, the Ottawas kept having to
travel farther into the wilderness in order to keep their
families fed between periods of trading. By the time
Pontiac reached adulthood, winters had become a time
of deprivation. The Indians' stores of preserved vegetables, meat, and fish were usually exhausted long before
the snows melted, and they were often forced to purchase
food from passing traders at exorbitant prices.

More lucrative trading took place in the spring, when
the Ottawas visited white settlements and bartered furs
for tools and food. Steel needles were in especially great
demand because they could mend tipis and leather
clothing without snapping in two as bone needles did.
The Europeans' wool and cotton fabrics were soft and
warm, and their steel knives and axes sturdy and sharp.
Muskets gained such popularity with the Indians that by
the 1760s the art of hunting with bows and arrows had
been almost completely forgotten. No matter how much
the Indians resented the Europeans' presence in their
country, they depended on the traders to provide them
with guns, powder, and bullets.

Much to the Indians' detriment, liquor was another
prized commodity. Rum and brandy had a strong effect
on the Indians, who before the arrival of the Europeans

had never been exposed to alcohol. As liquor came into common use in Indian villages, the Ottawas and other tribes faced problems they had never known before. Inebriated Indians quarreled with their neighbors, their conflicts often ending in violence. Unscrupulous traders plied the Indian hunters with rum in order to cheat them out of their furs. Indian leaders begged the whites to prohibit the sale of alcohol at trading posts, but such bans were disregarded by both traders and hunters.

Contact with traders brought the Indians another disaster: disease. Before the coming of Europeans, the Indians were generally healthy people whose only com-

Two Ottawa chiefs display their elaborate, silver-ornamented garments in an early 19th-century watercolor by Sir Joshua Jebb.

mon ailments were malnutrition and arthritis. Such scourges as smallpox, measles, tuberculosis, and syphilis were unknown until unwittingly spread by white traders. Entire Indian villages—even whole tribes—died in the resulting epidemics.

The European newcomers also affected the Indians' lives by involving them in their own wars. The Ottawas first participated in the European struggle for North America in 1744, when the French and British fought King George's War, named after Britain's King George II. At that time, both France and Britain had made claims on the North American continent. The French had set up their trading posts mainly in the northern regions, in what is now Canada; the British, meanwhile, had started farming colonies to the south along the Atlantic coast. As traders and settlers from both nations began moving toward the Ohio Valley, the two European powers eventually came to blows. Pontiac and his Ottawa warriors fought alongside the French, raiding British forts as well as the villages of Britain's Indian allies. The French were deemed the winners of this contest, but their victory did not bring an end to the British-French rivalry. In the uneasy peace that followed King George's War, each side built forts and enlisted Indian support in preparation for a new conflict.

By the mid-18th century, more than a million English colonists lived along the Atlantic coast. The French, meanwhile, who numbered perhaps 55,000 in 1754, controlled the interior of the continent. They built the fortress of Louisburg on present-day Cape Breton Island and founded settlements along the St. Lawrence River, around the Great Lakes, and all along the Mississippi River down to the French colony of New Orleans. The Indians of the Great Lakes region alone numbered as many as 70,000. The Indians' impressive population, along with their formidable prowess in battle, made them valuable allies for the side that was able to gain their support.

Far more tribes were befriended by the French than by the British. According to one trapper, the French colonial philosophy was "Those with whom we mingle do not become French, our people become Indian." French fur traders often adopted Indian clothing and customs, and some of them even took Indian wives. In contrast, British traders generally showed contempt for the Indians.

An English trader named Sir William Johnson was an exception to this rule. Johnson single-handedly enlisted the support of the mighty Iroquois confederation and even persuaded some of France's Indian allies to side with the British in the ongoing competition for control of the lucrative fur trade. Recognizing the potential that lay in a British-Indian alliance, he wrote, "Whoever pretends to say that the American savages are of little or no account to our interest on that continent, and that, therefore, it is not of great consequences, whether or no we endeavor to cultivate friendship with them, must be extremely ignorant, or else willfully perverse."

Known as Warraghiyagey (He-Who-Does-Much) by the Iroquois, Johnson acted as superintendent of Indian affairs for the northern colonies. The comfortable home he shared with his Mohawk wife, Molly Brant (sister of the renowned chief Joseph Brant), was frequently the center of negotiations and parleys between British and Indian leaders. A visiting soldier commented in his diary, "Sir Wm. continually plagued with Indians about him— generally 300–900 in number—spoil his garden and keep his house always dirty."

Most British officers were not so tolerant. Many regarded as "mercenary" the Indians' requests for food

and ammunition in exchange for military services. The young militia major George Washington, who was eventually to recruit countless Indian warriors to aid his regiment against the French, complained that they were "easily offended" and "greedy"—a common view among whites throughout the continent.

The Indians, meanwhile, had their own reservations about their European neighbors, French and British alike. C. F. Post, a missionary of the time, recorded the opinion

Indians and British soldiers gather for a council at Sir William Johnson Hall, near the Mohawk River in the British colony of New York. Johnson was one of the few British officials who believed in courting the favor of local tribes.

of a warrior who lived near him. "[The British] and the French are like the two edges of a pair of shears," said the Indian. "And we are the cloth which is cut to pieces between them."

Regiment d'Infanterie
Royal — Roussillon.

3

▽ ▽ ▽

THE RIVERS WILL RUN
WITH RUM

*This 1762 drawing shows a
French officer (right) and one
of his soldiers. From 1754 to
1760, the Ottawas and other
Great Lakes tribes fought
alongside the French in what
came to be known as the
French and Indian War.*

In the spring of 1754, Governor Robert Dinwiddie of the colony of Virginia ordered a party of local woodsmen to build a fort on the wedge of land where the Allegheny and Monongahela rivers converge with the mighty Ohio. From this vantage point, Dinwiddie reasoned, British scouts would be able to monitor all the traders who poled past in their flat-bottomed boats, or *bateaux*. The post would also allow the British to follow the movements of the Pennsylvania and Delaware Indians who traveled frequently along the three rivers.

One day, when the fort was still only partially built, the Virginians heard a shout from the nearby riverbank, and they soon discovered that more than 350 boats loaded with Indian warriors and French soldiers had landed on the beach. Realizing they were surrounded, the Virginians surrendered the fort without firing a shot and fled into the woods. The victorious French quickly completed the post and named it Fort Duquesne. Over the next several months, French soldiers continued to intercept British traders who tried to navigate past the fort's gates, eventually stopping nearly all of Britain's trade with the western Indians.

This was not the first indignity the British had suffered at the hands of the French. A few months earlier, the

Fort Duquesne, a military post begun by the British and completed by the French in 1754, overlooks a clearing near the forks of the Ohio River.

French army had built Fort Presqu'Isle on Lake Erie and pushed into the Ohio Valley, and French settlers and traders from the north—or *Canadiens,* as they were called—had begun claiming the rich farmland that spread across the region. Determined to put a stop to this invasion, Dinwiddie had dispatched 21-year-old adjutant general George Washington to meet with the French commander at Fort LeBoeuf and inform him that the Ohio Valley belonged to the British. Washington made the journey, and after a hospitable dinner, during which much wine was consumed, he was politely but firmly told that the French would imprison any British settler who crossed the Alleghenies into the Ohio Valley.

Soon after the French had stormed the British outpost on the forks of the Ohio, Dinwiddie decided it was time for action. In the spring of 1754, the governor put Washington in command of 120 soldiers and ordered him to capture Fort Duquesne. After a rigorous journey across the Allegheny Mountains, Washington's men halted at a place called Great Meadows on the Monongahela River. Exhausted and low on supplies, they built a small stockade, dubbed it Fort Necessity, and sent couriers back to Virginia, asking Dinwiddie to send reinforcements as quickly as possible.

Before help could arrive, however, Washington learned that a contingent of French soldiers was marching toward the fort where his troops had taken shelter. Enlisting the support of Half-King, a chief from the Mingo tribe, and a party of Mingo warriors, Washington set out to ambush the approaching French. The young officer launched the attack on a stormy night. Although it was his first military campaign, he remained undaunted by the bullets whistling past his head, later calling the experience "charming." The battle ended in a decisive victory for the British, initiating what came to be known as the French and Indian War.

Infuriated by this defeat, the French quickly retaliated. Nine hundred soldiers and their Indian allies attacked Fort Necessity on July 3, 1754, and a daylong barrage of gunfire left nearly half of Washington's men killed or wounded. By the end of the siege, Washington was forced to cede Britain's claims to the Ohio Valley.

But the war did not end with this engagement. The French had tasted victory, and now they were determined to win the continent. Calling themselves the Indians' "champions against the English," they quickly recruited some 20 tribes to their cause. An English hostage at Fort Duquesne described the way the French wooed and won the warrior Shamokin Daniel:

> [The French] presented him with a laced coat and hat, a blanket, shirts, ribbons, a new gun, powder, lead etc. When he returned he was quite changed, and said, "See here, you fools, what the French have given me. I was [with the British] and never received a farthing. The English are fools, and so are you."

The British, meanwhile, were hardly ready to capitulate. Early in 1755, Edward Braddock, an arrogant and
unimaginative British general, was given a command of
2,500 men and ordered to make a second attempt at
capturing Fort Duquesne. The fort now held a mere 300
French regulars. Camped in their vicinity, however, were
more than 800 Ottawa Indians, together with a large force
of Ojibwas, Potawatomis, Abnakis, Caughnawagas,
Hurons, Delawares, and Shawnees. Although historians
differ on this point, some believe the Ottawa party was
led by Pontiac.

A French scout informed the fort's commander, Pierre
de Contrecoeur, that Braddock's army was on its way.
Knowing his men were heavily outnumbered by the
English, de Contrecoeur prepared to surrender, but his
daring adjutant, Daniel de Beaujeu, intervened and
proposed a bold maneuver. The commander gave his
reluctant consent.

Working fast, de Beaujeu rallied 200 French soldiers
and 600 Indians and instructed them to fan out into the
woods above the Monongahela River. Braddock's troops
had just forded the river when they heard the first rifle
shots ring out. De Beaujeu's men were so well hidden
that it seemed to the British as if the volleys of bullets
were coming from rocks and trees. Trained to fight a
uniformed and visible foe, the British soldiers panicked.
Close to a thousand of them were killed or wounded in
three hours. According to Charles Stuart, a British man
captured and held prisoner by the Ottawas, in the bloody
aftermath of battle the Ottawas perpetrated "shocking
atrocities" against their captives. Stuart claimed that
Pontiac's reputation as a fierce and unforgiving warrior
was linked to this savagery.

News of Braddock's defeat outraged British settlers on
the Atlantic seaboard. In England, meanwhile, the British

man of letters Horace Walpole referred to the conflict as "the longest battle that ever was fought with nobody."

Defeated in the Ohio Valley, the British decided to shift the focus of their operations to the Great Lakes region. There too, however, they were soon outwitted, this time thanks to the gifted French strategist the Marquis de Montcalm and his Ottawa, Ojibwa, and Potawatomi allies.

As the war progressed, the British began to appreciate the tremendous fighting power wielded by their enemy's Indian warriors. Sir William Johnson wrote, "Without any exaggeration, I look upon the Northern Indians to be the most formidable of any uncivilized body of people in the world. Hunting and war are their sole occupation, and the one qualifies them for the other." Similarly, George Washington commented publicly that "the French grow more and more formidable by their alliances [with the northern Indians], while our friendly Indians are deserting our interest."

Of the tribes who sided with the French, the Ottawas enjoyed a special reputation both for their loyalty and for their love of battle. Aiding Montcalm at Lake George in July 1756, the Ottawas surprised 300 British soldiers who were transporting 22 barges of supplies to nearby Fort William Henry. According to Montcalm's report, 160 British soldiers were "killed, drowned or put to the torture" and 151 taken prisoner. Only one Ottawa warrior died in the skirmish.

A year later, on August 3, 1757, Montcalm led a force of 6,200 regulars and 1,800 Indians—30 of them from Pontiac's village—to attack Fort William Henry itself. Six days later, the fort surrendered. Montcalm guaranteed the inhabitants' safe passage to the nearest British post, but the Indians were infuriated by these terms. They had fought hard in the battle and felt they were being cheated out of their rewards of scalps and loot. When the English prisoners, escorted by a few French guards, reached a place in the road just out of sight of the fort, the Indians leapt from the woods, tomahawks and war clubs in hand. As many as 250 men and women were killed or captured before Montcalm's soldiers managed to intervene. The marquis was disgusted by this "dishonorable" act; it marked the first breach in relations between the French and the Indians.

Just as a British surrender seemed eminent, the tide began to turn against the French. On July 26, 1758, the great fortress at Louisburg in present-day Nova Scotia fell to 1,200 British regulars under Lord Jeffrey Amherst. A month later, 12,000 British regulars captured Fort Frontenac—present-day Kingston, Ontario—and gained control of Lake Ontario at the source of the St. Lawrence River.

Encouraged by these victories, the cautious and capable General John Forbes set out to take the Ohio Valley from the French. His army moved forward with care, building defensive stockades as it went. Forbes's effort was stymied in September 1758, when he sent some 800 Scottish Highlanders to scout around Fort Duquesne and a third of them were killed in a skirmish with Indian forces. Yet the Indians, too, sustained a large number of casualties in this engagement, and in the end the fort fell to the British. Demoralized, the Indians began to desert the French cause.

The British seized this belated opportunity to win the Indians over to their side. Sir William Johnson met with a delegation of Delawares, Shawnees, and Mingos, while the trader George Croghan, a skillful mediator, invited Pontiac and other Ottawa chiefs to the former Fort Duquesne, now called Fort Pitt (the original site of Pittsburgh, Pennsylvania). Croghan promised the Ottawas that "the rivers would run with rum and that

British troops under General John Forbes prepare to take Fort Duquesne in the fall of 1758.

trade goods would be . . . plentiful and cheap" if they supported the British. Later, Pontiac reported these bribes to the French, boasting that he could not be influenced by such "evil suggestions."

Meanwhile, Sir William Johnson promised the Delawares that their home in the Susquehanna Valley, which had been overrun by white settlers, would be returned to them. Johnson also declared that the lands west of the Appalachians would be given back to the tribes that had lost them in wars with the Iroquois, who were Britain's most loyal ally. So successful were these parleys that the French were soon fighting most of the very tribes they had once counted as friends. Only a small band of Ottawas, perhaps influenced by Pontiac, remained loyal to the French cause. Legend has it that Montcalm rewarded Pontiac for his fealty by presenting the war chief with one of his own dress uniforms.

Soon Forts Pitt, Frontenac, Louisburg, Niagara, and Ticonderoga were all in British hands. In September 1759, British troops under General James Wolfe faced the Marquis de Montcalm's regulars on the Plains of Abraham outside the walled Canadian city of Quebec. Both commanders were killed on that bloody day, but General Wolfe lived long enough to know that a British victory had been won.

The British moved quickly to consolidate their gains. George Croghan met with 24 Ottawa, Delaware, and Shawnee leaders to secure their cooperation with the new regime. The chiefs ceremonially buried a hatchet—a symbol of war—under a pine tree. The Ottawa chief Mehemah said on this occasion, "Some years ago the French got the better of our understanding and by the assistance of the Evil Spirit put the hatchet into our hands,

The Death of Wolfe, a celebrated 1771 painting by American artist Benjamin West, shows British general James Wolfe mortally stricken at the Battle of Quebec on September 13, 1759. Wolfe's opposite number, French commander Marquis Louis Joseph de Montcalm, also died in the fight for the city, which—along with the rest of Canada—fell to the British on September 18.

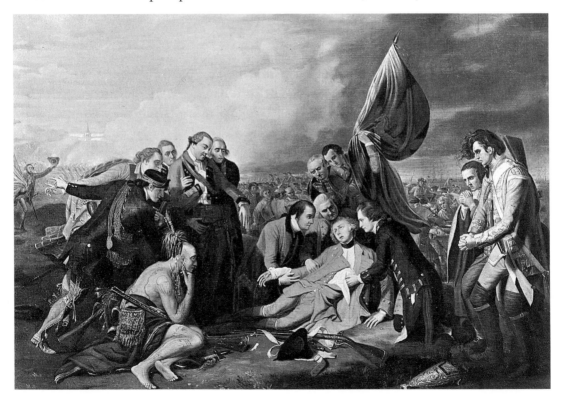

which we were foolish enough to make use of against our brothers, the English." Mehemah swore that his people would never fight the British again.

A year later the British laid siege to Montreal. The French governor of the city surrendered to General Amherst, commander of His Majesty's forces in North America, on September 8, 1760. The French conceded several forts on the Great Lakes as well, most notably Detroit and Michilimackinac. The day after the surrender of Montreal, General Amherst sent Major Robert Rogers and his company of rangers to take possession of these posts.

Rogers, a bold explorer and woodsman, arrived at the mouth of the Chogage River near Fort Detroit on November 7, 1760. In his book *A Concise Account of North America*, he wrote,

> I was met in my way by an embassy from [Pontiac], of some of his warriors, and some of the chiefs of the tribes that are under him; the purport of which was, to let me know, that Ponteack [sic] was at a small distance, coming peaceably, and that he desired me to halt my detachment till such time as he could see me with his own eyes. His ambassadors had also orders to inform me, that he was Ponteack, the King and Lord of the country I was in.

A short while later Pontiac appeared, displaying what Rogers called "an air of majesty and princely grandeur." "Why are you trespassing in my lands?" Pontiac demanded with an assurance the captain described as "far from [that] of a conquered Prince." Rogers deferentially informed Pontiac that the French had been defeated and he was on his way to raise the British flag over Fort Detroit. Pontiac received this information impassively. Just as suddenly as he had arrived, he left the rangers' camp.

The British soldiers remained on their guard all through that night, expecting an attack. None occurred.

In the morning, however, Pontiac returned with his retinue of braves. With great ceremony, the war chief announced that he would live peacefully beside his new English neighbors as long as they treated him "with the respect and honour due to a King or Emperor." But if he or his people were mistreated, Pontiac warned, he would put the British in their place by cutting off their route to the interior. He offered Rogers the red calumet—the pipe of peace—and promised to send "to the several Indian towns on the south-side and west-end of Lake Erie, to inform them that I had his consent to come into the country." Rogers was impressed by the war chief's "strength of judgement, and thirst after knowledge," as well as his obvious influence over the Great Lakes tribes.

On November 29, 1760, the French flag came down at Fort Detroit. Rogers left Captain Donald Campbell, a kindly, plump, and near-sighted officer, in charge and set off for Fort Michilimackinac. He dispatched other officers

Pontiac and a small party of followers meet Major Robert Rogers and his rangers at the end of the French and Indian War. Impressed by the war chief's proud demeanor, Rogers also noted that Pontiac was "greatly honored and revered by his subjects."

to take possession of Fort Miami on Lake Erie and Fort Ouiatenon on the Ohio River.

The change in command did not immediately affect the French settlers, or *habitants,* who farmed and hunted along the banks of the Detroit River. Captain Campbell was welcomed hospitably and invited to many lively gatherings and card parties by the convivial French. But there was one policy that the new regime changed. Campbell was under stringent orders to restrict the sale of gunpowder and bullets to the Indians.

The French had always given presents of ammunition and provisions to the natives in order to secure their cooperation in the alliance against the English. The Indians actually considered such gifts a form of land rent. General Amherst, however, believed that if presents were made, there would be "no end to giving." He told his subordinates,

> I am not for giving [the Indians] any provisions; when they find they can get it on asking for, they will grow remiss in their hunting, which must industriously be avoided; for so long as their minds are intent on business they will not have leisure to hatch mischief. Nothing could be so impolitic as to furnish them with the means of accomplishing the evil which is so much dreaded. Services must be rewarded, but as to purchasing the good behavior either of Indians or any others, I do not understand. When men of whatsoever race behave ill, they must be punished not bribed.

The effects of this policy were felt immediately, as the Indians began to run out of ammunition for hunting. Pontiac may have realized that with the French defeated, the British no longer feared—or needed—the Indians, and the conquerors had not hesitated to offend their erstwhile allies. In the words of General Amherst, the Indians were now nothing more to the British than an "expensive nuisance."

4

"SOMETHING NOT RIGHT IS BREWING"

On an autumn day in 1762, Sir William Johnson could be found at home on his beautiful Mohawk Valley estate, preparing a report for General Amherst. "I am very apprehensive that something not right is brewing," he wrote. A trusted Iroquois had told him of rumors circulating among the Shawnees and Delawares: unless relations between the British and Indians improved, the Indians intended to launch a bloody insurrection.

Johnson needed to convince Amherst that the French custom of giving gifts to the tribes should continue. As Johnson understood it, it was part of Indian tradition for a host to share everything he or she owned with visitors. When a visiting warrior walked into a fort, he expected to be given whatever food, clothing, or gunpowder he required. By withholding these gifts, the British were insulting and angering their new allies. For months Johnson had spent his own money to feed and clothe Indians who visited his estate. Meanwhile, Amherst had steadfastly refused to look at the situation from the Indians' point of view. So convinced was he that these "insatiable animals" posed no threat to the British that he had forbidden Johnson to give them anything more.

Sir William Johnson, whose diplomatic efforts won the Iroquois over to the British cause, tried hard to persuade the British army to honor the gift-giving tradition begun by French traders. Few British officers, however, shared Johnson's commitment to cordial British-Indian relations.

47

By the Honorable Sir William Johnson Bar.t His Majesty's sole Agent and Super-Intendant of Indian Affairs for the Northern Depart-ment of North America. Colonel of the Six United Nations their Allies and Dependants &c. &c.

To

Whereas I have received repeated proofs of your Attachment to his Britanic Majesty's Interests, and Zeal for his Service upon Sundry occasions, more particularly

I do therefore give you this public Testimonial thereof as a proof of his Majesty's Esteem & Approba-tion, Declaring you the said   to be a   of Your   and recommending it to all his Majesty's Subjects and faithfull Indian Allies to Treat and Consider you upon all occasions agreable to your Character. Station, and Services. _____

Given under my Hand and Seal at Arms at Johnson hall the   day of   '7

By Command of Sir W. Johnson

George Croghan, Johnson's colleague in negotiations with the tribes, was even more worried. That fall he reported to Amherst that the western tribes were telling all who would listen that the British planned to kill the Indians and steal their land for settlements as soon as all the white captives in Indian hands had been recovered.

As part of his goodwill policy, William Johnson gave this certificate, together with a medal, to Indian chiefs who showed outstanding loyalty to the British cause.

Croghan wrote, "I dread the event [of violence] as I know Indians can't long persevere [under these conditions]. They are a rash, inconsistent people and inclined to mischief." Yet Amherst remained convinced that his Indian policy was just and fair. Believing that the various Indian tribes were too hostile toward each other to unite under a single leader and thus could never be a potent military threat, he disregarded Croghan's warnings.

Johnson knew his report would probably go unheeded; meanwhile, a letter he received from Captain Campbell at Fort Detroit caused his alarm to grow. It was clear that the captain shared Johnson's fears. Campbell wrote, "I hope that the general will change his present way of thinking with regard to Indian affairs. As I am of the opinion if they were supplied with ammunition it would prevent their doing mischief."

Campbell spoke the Ottawa language, and he had heard firsthand that the Indians' situation was desperate. Their economy, based on the fur trade, had been ruined by the French and Indian War, and they expected compensation for the many tribesmen they had lost in the fighting. The Indians' fields had lain fallow while they pursued the war. They had no seeds to plant and no ammunition for hunting. They looked to the British for help, and none was forthcoming. To add to the Indians' misery, traders at the wilderness outposts had raised the price of food and bullets.

Campbell had watched the Indians' complaints gradually turn into threats. He wondered how tribal leaders might react if they learned that a new fort was being constructed on Lake Erie. Not only had Amherst attempted to keep the project a secret from the neighboring Hurons, but in so doing he had refused to offer the tribe any compensation for the use of their land.

Campbell believed there was only one man who might

A Potawatomi warrior stands ready for battle. The Potawatomis, who were among the Ottawas' closest allies, joined forces with Pontiac in the early 1760s.

be able to ease the trouble that was brewing: the Ottawa war chief Pontiac. Pontiac was the chief of three Ottawa villages in the vicinity of Fort Detroit, and his advice on British-Indian relations was also sought by the Ojibwas and the Potawatomis. Campbell liked and respected the war chief, partly because Pontiac was openly curious about such modern technologies as the manufacture of iron and cloth, as well as the details of British military discipline. Campbell also noticed that Pontiac seemed to be traveling a great deal. According to canadien inform-ants, the Indian leader was visiting native villages throughout the Great Lakes region. It was still not too late for the British to right past wrongs before a rebellion broke out, and Campbell hoped to recruit Pontiac's help in this endeavor.

What Campbell did not realize was that Pontiac's recent activities were all directed toward shoring up support for the coming insurrection. Pontiac planned a rebellion on a scale never before attempted in North America, and he was proceeding shrewdly, with caution and deliberation. So far he had persuaded Ninivois, the Potawatomi chief, and Takee, chief of the Hurons, to join him. He had called for a council to be attended by the tribes of the Great Lakes as well as the more distant Ojibwas and Ottawas.

Having experienced the bloody realities of war, Pontiac knew that his only chance of victory against the British lay in an alliance of all the Great Lakes Indian tribes, with material support from the French. The French commander in Illinois—which was still French territory—had recently declared himself willing to supply the war chief with guns and ammunition. Many of the Canadiens living along the Detroit River hoped that King Louis's armies would soon be on the move again, marching north from Louisiana to fight at Pontiac's side.

British-Indian relations worsened in October 1762, when a strange sulfurous black rain fell on Fort Detroit. The soldiers playfully tried to use the bad-smelling stuff for ink, but Pontiac, who by this time had come under the influence of Neolin, the so-called Delaware Prophet, warned his people that it marked the fort as a place of evil.

Wampum belts calling for an attack on Fort Detroit were circulated among the Delawares, Ottawas, and Potawatomis. Within a few months, the Mohawks, Senecas, Shawnees, and Oneidas had also declared themselves ready to fight. Major Gladwin, the new commander of

Fort Detroit, paid informants to keep him abreast of Pontiac's activities.

The stage for rebellion was set when Pontiac's secret council drew some 20,000 Indians to the banks of the Ecorse River at the end of April 1763. A little more than a week later, on May 7, Pontiac's warriors gained admittance to Fort Detroit, secretly ready to mount their first attack. Unfortunately for the Indians, Gladwin and Campbell had been informed of the plan by spies; the enterprise was foiled. Pontiac wisely chose to retreat, but the incident only fueled his decision to launch a full-scale war against the British.

The Indians' first savage blow was struck two days after the incident at Fort Detroit. Pontiac's warriors attacked and scalped three whites in the cabin of a settler

Pontiac addresses a council near Fort Detroit. In April 1763, as many as 20,000 Indians from all around the Great Lakes and the Ohio Valley gathered to hear him speak on the banks of the Ecorse River.

named Mrs. Turnbull, within full sight of Fort Detroit. A soldier who stood on the ramparts described the Ottawas as "yelping like so many devils" as they descended on the Turnbull home. While Gladwin and Campbell watched helplessly, the warriors raced from the site of the attack to the shores of the Detroit River, leapt into their canoes, and paddled to Isle-au-Cochon, where they murdered and scalped five more people. The war had begun.

All was confusion in Pontiac's village as women frantically packed their families' possessions for a move to a safer place upriver. Within a few hours even the bark roofs of the longhouses were ready to be transported. Darkness fell, and Pontiac, in full war paint and ceremonial regalia, began to dance before the fire. In a high, wailing voice he sang of his exploits in battle and the vengeance he would wreak upon the British. The warriors of the village enthusiastically joined him in the war dance, and the chilly evening air was filled with their songs.

Later that night, the Ottawas moved their village to the mouth of Parent Creek—soon to be renamed Bloody Run. Here, Pontiac was greeted by a band of Ojibwas from the Bay of Saginaw. He could now summon a total of 460 warriors for his attack on Fort Detroit.

The next day, tidings of further Indian attacks reached the frightened soldiers at the fort. Two English officers had been murdered north of Lake St. Clair. According to reports, one man had been boiled and eaten, and the skin of his forearm had been tanned for use as a tobacco pouch. Threatening howls were soon heard outside the fort's palisades. A swarm of Wyandots, Potawatomis, and Ojibwas had crept up close to the fort, concealed themselves behind fallen trees and abandoned outbuildings, and begun a rapid barrage of musket fire. The shooting continued relentlessly for more than six hours.

Throughout all of this, Gladwin remained undaunted. He felt sure that the Indians would find themselves in need of food and ammunition and be willing to parley before the week was out. Accordingly, he sent a canadien interpreter named La Butte to Pontiac's village to offer terms of peace.

La Butte found the Indians receptive and quickly delivered Gladwin's message. The commander of Fort Detroit, he told them, promised he would do his best to redress their grievances if they would end the fighting. Pontiac sat cross-legged on a woven mat, smoking his pipe and nodding impassively. Hopeful that the negotiations would be successful, La Butte soon returned to the fort to inform Gladwin of the evening's progress. On his second visit to the Ottawa village, however, he discovered that no terms had been reached. Pontiac refused to have his men lay down their arms. Finally, after a conference with his chiefs, he demanded that the British leaders consult with him in person.

Despite Gladwin's suspicions, Campbell agreed to meet with Pontiac face to face. The captain and his companion, Lieutenant George McDougall, had no sooner stepped through the gates of the fort than they were met by an habitant named Monsieur Gouin who lived near the new Ottawa village. Gouin was certain that the Indians were preparing for a long war and that this peace parley was only a ruse. Campbell refused to be dissuaded.

Campbell and McDougall had just crossed the narrow wooden bridge over Parent Creek when they found themselves surrounded by a mob of Indians, whooping and howling ferociously. Yet in a few minutes Pontiac parted the crowd, silenced his people with a gesture, and led the two men to the village council house. No sooner had the white men seated themselves than a crowd of curious Indians gathered all around them. Campbell cleared his throat and addressed the war chief:

My brother, Chief Pontiac, knows me; he knows that when I speak to him, I speak from my heart and that I have not told him lies. I know that you have had an anger in your heart, but to declare war against us is not the way to settle any differences. All over this country there are forts in which there are English soldiers, and the farther to the east one goes, the more of them there are. If you continue in the way you have begun, so many soldiers will spill from the east into this country that they could not be counted and one by one they will destroy villages and warriors until peace is made again or there are no Indians left. Will my brother, Pontiac, not now tell me that the fires of anger have cooled; and will my brother, Pontiac, not now come to the fort with us to talk with Major Gladwin and settle whatever difficulties he feels exist between us?

Campbell's speech was answered by an hour-long hostile silence. At length, the captain stood and expressed his desire to return to Fort Detroit. Pontiac refused to let him go. "My father," he said, addressing the captain, "will sleep tonight in the lodges of his red children." Campbell realized that he and McDougall were captives. The siege of Fort Detroit would continue, and the two officers would be used as bargaining chips.

Pontiac's determination to take Fort Detroit mirrored his ability to organize and inspire Indian warriors from all around the Great Lakes region. He could use the captive officers not only to manipulate the British but also to impress other Indian tribes with his power and cunning. Indeed, the day after Campbell's capture, the Wyandot tribe was persuaded to join the siege.

Pontiac continued to formulate his battle plan. He directed one band of Potawatomis to prevent any British ships from approaching Fort Detroit by river. A second band was sent to scout the forests surrounding the fort, cutting off any reinforcements that might come by land. A third band watched the fort day and night, taking potshots at soldiers who lifted their heads above the battlements.

REGIMENT   REGIMENT   REGIMENT

Significantly, although Pontiac had declared war on the British, he had never ordered his warriors to fight. According to Indian custom, if a warrior preferred to refrain from battle, he was free to stay at home. In contrast to British soldiers, who enlisted for a certain period of time and were subject to court-martial if they abandoned their duties during that period, Indian warriors could resign from battle at any time without shame or punishment. Pontiac's power, therefore, lay not in a military system but in the respect he was able to inspire in his followers. Had it not been for this respect, he would not have been permitted to lead.

When the war parties of many tribes united to form a single army, it was common for the chiefs of the different tribes to elect one warrior to serve as their leader,

British grenadiers display their uniforms in a 1751 painting by David Morier.

and in this respect Pontiac's position was not unusual. However, if any of the tribal chiefs disagreed with the head chief's decisions, they would simply disregard his authority. Such a strong regard for individual choice made long military actions almost impossible for the Indians to sustain. Banking on this characteristic of Native American combat, Amherst had declared an operation on the scale of Pontiac's rebellion infeasible. Pontiac had proved him wrong: he had unified thousands of Indian warriors of many different tribes under his own leadership and was methodically conducting a sustained military assault.

Pontiac also had every confidence in his ability to lead his warriors to victory. But the war chief did not yet realize that his greatest obstacle was not the 25-foot-high walls of Fort Detroit, or even the fort's deadly cannon, but rather its stalwart and stubborn commanding officer, Major Henry Gladwin.

5

BESIEGED

Meeting Gladwin in his private office, a small group of Canadiens nervously delivered a message from the Ottawa encampment where Campbell and McDougall were being held prisoner. The message, dictated by Pontiac and transcribed by Campbell, declared that unless the commander surrendered Fort Detroit, an army of 1,500 Indians would attack not only the British army but also every white settlement—French and British alike— for miles around.

To Gladwin, the bearers of the message were further proof of Pontiac's cunning. The war chief was deliberately using the habitants as go-betweens. Many of the Canadiens sympathized with the Ottawas and hated British rule. Others merely feared for the lives of their families and the existence of their farms. Gladwin knew he had to resist Pontiac to the bitter end. He also knew that the habitants would, for self-preservation, support whoever won this battle of wills. He politely refused to surrender, and the Canadiens departed.

Not one hour later, 600 Indian warriors attacked Fort Detroit. After 12 hours of fighting, a Canadien once again approached the fort with a message from Pontiac. If Gladwin would capitulate, the war chief promised, his

Major Henry Gladwin, a cool-headed veteran of the French and Indian War, took command of Fort Detroit in 1761. He was 34 years old when the post was besieged by Pontiac's forces.

soldiers would be granted safe passage to Fort Niagara. Again Gladwin refused.

Many of the commander's officers pressed him to reconsider. The Indian band was 10 to 15 times larger than the white population in and around Fort Detroit. The garrison had few provisions and little ammunition. Many of the houses and stores within the fort's walls were made of wood and could be easily ignited by arrows twisted with burning straw.

Gladwin remained immovable. The fractious Indians would soon begin to argue among themselves and disperse, he insisted. Instead of surrendering, he instructed his officers to focus on the immediate problem of securing

A 25-foot-tall stockade surrounds Fort Detroit, the largest British post on the western frontier. This view shows the western entrance and a path leading to the river.

food and ammunition. He ordered the habitants within the stockade to add their food to the common supplies and informed the settlers who lived along the river that they too needed to contribute to the army's stores.

Under cover of darkness, a small band of men crept through the stockade's gates to burn down barns and cut down trees that the Indians used for cover. Two schooners that were anchored in the Detroit River, the *Huron* and the *Michigan*, began firing their cannons at Pontiac's warriors, preventing them from approaching the fort from that direction. Barrels of rainwater were placed in the fort's drill square to use against fires caused by burning arrows. The attacks continued. Traders and soldiers stood side by side on the ramparts under Gladwin's watchful eye.

Meanwhile, according to historian Allan W. Eckert, Pontiac met with habitant leaders at his village, telling them,

> We are sorely lacking in supplies, especially powder and ball. You have such supplies and you will turn them over to me. If you do not do so willingly, then you will suffer the pain of having them plundered from you, and I would not wish to see any of you hurt. Don't hold back or keep supplies from me, but give them freely. You will be paid for their worth.

Pontiac had two other requests of the French settlers. He wanted them to teach him how to dig European-style entrenchments, a series of ditches that would give his warriors cover as they attacked the fort. He also wanted them to join in the siege against the British defenders of Fort Detroit. The habitants were just as afraid of British retribution as they were of the Indians, however, and they refused to take part in the fighting.

Frustrated but not discouraged, Pontiac was determined to make Fort Detroit surrender before the Indian confederation ran out of supplies. Again he composed a message to Major Gladwin. Unless the fort was surrendered, he said, it would be taken by force, and all those found within its walls would be tortured to death.

Gladwin sent a bold reply. He had not been assigned to command Fort Detroit only to turn it and its contents over to the Indians, he declared. Furthermore, even if he were inclined to surrender, he would not do so as long as Pontiac held Campbell and McDougall prisoner. Sardonically, Gladwin advised Pontiac to save his ammunition for hunting.

On May 14, a delegation of habitants entered Pontiac's village and complained that the Indians were stealing their crops and livestock. The fur trade was completely disrupted, and they were being ruined by the siege. "If you wish relief," Pontiac replied, "then you have only to join me and all the fighting will end that much faster." But again the French-speaking settlers refused, and Pontiac sent them away.

By this time, the war had been going on for a week. Pontiac's forces had killed 15 English men and women, wounded 5, and captured 15. No Indians had been killed, but their food stores were already nearly exhausted. Time, at least, seemed to be on Pontiac's side. His Indian allies along the Great Lakes knew of his attacks and were planning some of their own. Many other tribes had made their way to the Detroit River to join the campaign, and their combined forces were indeed formidable. Pontiac's army now included the 250 Ottawas under his own command, 150 Potawatomis led by Chief Ninivois, 50 Wyandots under Chief Takee, 200 Ojibwas led by Wasson, and another 170 Ojibwas commanded by Chief Sekahos. These warriors had brought their families with them, and so there were now more than 3,000 Indians camped in the woods near Fort Detroit.

On May 15, Pontiac and four Ottawa chiefs visited the

settlers along the shores of the Detroit River and demanded food. Pontiac had decided that the habitants would supply his warriors with provisions for the rest of the campaign. The Ottawas, according to his plan, would be fed by the settlers who lived north and east of the fort; the Potawatomis would receive supplies of food from those living to the southwest; the Hurons would be provided for by settlers living across the Detroit River. The Indian leaders explained to the settlers that they would be paid for their help, giving them promissory notes of birch bark bearing Pontiac's mark, a raccoon, for every item of food taken. Some Ottawa women were sent to help the Canadiens tend their fields, and the Indians were warned that anyone caught stealing would be publicly punished.

This newest demonstration of Pontiac's ability to organize large groups of people to benefit his cause was soon relayed to Major Gladwin, who could only admit a grudging respect for the war chief. The English commander had begun to recognize the tremendous power of his adversary.

Pontiac, meanwhile, began to reassess his strategy. He realized that in order to take Fort Detroit and keep it, he would have to go beyond the traditional methods of Indian warfare—he needed European expertise. Pontiac summoned Campbell and asked him to write a letter to the French in Illinois, requesting a military officer who could act as commandant of Fort Detroit once the British were driven out. Once again, Campbell wrote down Pontiac's dictation:

> Listen, you French brethren, who are prisoners [of the British] as well as we. All that the Delawares and Shawnees told us is now come to pass. The Delawares told us this spring that the English sought to become masters of all and would put us to death. They told us also, "Our brethren, let

us die together, since the design of the English is to destroy us. We are dead one way or another." When we saw this, we decided to say to all the nations who are your children to fall in here at Detroit, which they have done. We pray our father at the Illinois to hasten to come to our succor.

Pontiac signed his letters to Gladwin with this mark.

Indian runners took the letter, along with wampum war belts for the Indians near Forts Miami and Ouiatenon, and set off at top speed on the long journey to Illinois.

Meanwhile, the siege of Fort Detroit continued. When Gladwin dispatched one of his ships to Niagara to request supplies and reinforcements from the British fort there, Pontiac's warriors manned their canoes. Campbell was placed in the prow of the leading craft, functioning as a kind of human shield, and the Indians set out to attack the huge ship. A strong wind quickly bore the ship away, however, and the Indians could not paddle fast enough to follow.

On May 30, a line of bateaux was sighted from the battlements of Fort Detroit, and the British troops let out great cheers of relief to learn that reinforcements were so close at hand. One sharp-eyed soldier, however, gave a cry of despair. The boats were commanded not by Englishmen but by Indians. Soon enough, the soldiers' shouts of joy were echoed across the water by war whoops.

The convoy, which contained supplies for all the British forts in the Great Lakes region, had been captured by a band of Wyandots. In each of the eight bateaux, captured soldiers rowed under the watchful eyes of several Indian warriors. Other warriors followed alongside the flat-bottomed boats in birch bark canoes, and still more Indians ran along the riverbanks. As the lead boat neared Fort Detroit, the distraught faces of the soldiers held captive in the bateaux deeply impressed the soldiers watching from the fort's ramparts.

Suddenly, a prisoner attacked one of the Wyandot warriors guarding his boat and tried to push him into the river. The Indian kept a firm grip on the man's clothes and reached for his dagger, stabbing the sailor repeatedly until they both fell overboard. The other Wyandots who had been guarding the boat leapt into the water to aid their comrade, and the soldiers who had been under their command seized the opportunity to head for shore. Cannon fire burst from the warship that remained anchored in the river outside the fort. The escaping soldiers managed to elude both the Indians' swift canoes and the bullets whistling overhead; they saved seven barrels of provisions and gunpowder for the British.

The rest of the supplies sent from Niagara were taken in triumph to Pontiac's village. That night, the inhabitants of Fort Detroit heard terrible cries coming from the beach. The soldiers who had manned the remaining bateaux were being tortured to death with great ceremony.

On June 2, Pontiac resolved to capture the smaller British forts on the Great Lakes and sent a fleet of canoes carrying 200 men down the Detroit River to Lake Huron.

Soon after capture of the relief convoy, the disheartened residents of Fort Detroit learned that Fort Sandusky, on the southern shore of Lake Huron, had fallen to the Indians. The commander of that fort, Ensign Christopher Paully, had been taken prisoner by the Wyandots and adopted by a widowed Wyandot woman. Granted all the privileges of tribal membership, Paully had managed to get a letter to Gladwin describing the fort's siege.

Unaware of Pontiac's rebellion, Paully had walked blindly into the war chief's trap. On May 16, seven Wyandots had requested a meeting with him at Fort Sandusky. He had asked the men into his office, where they had lit the peace pipe and settled in as if to discuss an important matter. Then, without warning, they had leapt up, seized Paully, and dragged him onto the fort's parade ground, where he was forced to watch as the soldiers under his command were massacred.

Fort Sandusky was only one of the British military posts taken by Pontiac's allies that month. Gladwin soon learned that an Indian war party had occupied Fort St. Joseph (present-day Niles, Michigan), an outpost originally founded by the French in the swamps of the St. Joseph River, near the head of Lake Michigan. On June 15, a band of Potawatomis escorted three of the post's survivors to the gates of Fort Detroit, where they were able to exchange their prisoners for comrades captured by the British. Once inside the protective walls of Fort Detroit, Ensign Francis Schlosser, the defeated commander of Fort St. Joseph, told his tale to Gladwin.

On the morning of May 25, Schlosser's garrison had seen an increase in traffic on the St. Joseph River. Apparently, the local Potawatomis were being visited by cousins from another village. The visitors' chief, Washashe, came to Schlosser's quarters to offer his greetings. Before Schlosser could respond, a Canadien ran

Ojibwas engage in a spirited ballgame outside northern Michigan's Fort Michilimackinac. Midway through the game, the Indians stormed the fort and massacred dozens of soldiers.

into the room shouting, "Watch out! I think they mean trouble."

Schlosser ran across the parade ground to the barracks, which were thronged with friendly-looking Potawatomis. As he called to his 14 soldiers to arm themselves, the warriors' expression suddenly changed. They rushed to the gates, tomahawked the sentinel, and opened the way for a large band of Indians waiting outside to enter. Within minutes the fort was plundered and 11 soldiers were killed. The three survivors, Schlosser among them, were bound hand and foot and eventually brought to Fort Detroit.

Just three days later, a letter arrived from Captain Etherington of Fort Michilimackinac, at the northern tip of Michigan's lower peninsula, informing Gladwin that his garrison had fallen into the hands of the Ojibwas. "The Chippeways [Ojibwas] who live in a plain near this fort assembled to play ball," the letter read. "They played from morning till noon; then, throwing their ball close to the gate, and observing Lieutenant Lesley and me a few paces out of it, they came behind us, seized and carried us into the woods."

Other Ojibwas had rushed into the fort, where the Ojibwa women had already gathered, their weapons concealed under the blankets they wore about their shoulders. The resulting massacre was vividly described by Alexander Henry, a young English trader who witnessed the scene from a hiding place:

> Through an aperture which afforded me a view of the area of the fort, I beheld, in shapes the foulest and most horrible, the ferocious triumphs of barbarian conquerors. The dead were scalped and mangled; the dying were writhing and shrieking under the unsatiated knife and tomahawk; and from the bodies of some, ripped open, their butchers were drinking the blood, scooped up in the hollow of joined hands and quaffed amid shouts of rage and victory.

After Detroit, Fort Michilimackinac was the most important fort on the Great Lakes. The striking similarity between the trick the Ojibwas used to gain entrance to it and Pontiac's original plan to take Fort Detroit suggests that the Ojibwas acted with Pontiac's strategy in mind.

Finally, on the morning of July 2, Gladwin received some hopeful news from Europe. The Treaty of Paris had at last been signed, ending the Seven Years' War between France and Great Britain. Under its terms the French lost all their possessions in North America except for two tiny islands off the coast of Newfoundland. The commander of Fort Detroit could now be confident that, despite Pontiac's entreaties, the French garrisons in Illinois would not be fighting at the Indians' side. Pontiac and his Indian allies were on their own.

6

"A DAMN'D DRUBBING"

As the siege of Fort Detroit dragged on through the month of June, Major Gladwin walked along the ramparts each night. Staring into the darkness, he could see little except the peaceful gleam of moonlight on the flowing river. It was quiet, but he knew that just beyond the walls, mortal danger lurked. When he turned and looked out over the battlements, he saw nearly a hundred small thatched houses and four sturdy blockhouses. The barracks, the council house, and a small church hugged the fort's 25-foot walls. About 120 soldiers and 40 armed trappers were with him defending the fort. The *Huron* and the *Michigan* lay anchored offshore.

Privately, Gladwin admitted what his officers had asserted again and again: his resources were severely limited. Gladwin did not have enough cannons to arm every corner of the fort, and, more significantly, he did not have enough provisions to feed the fort's defenders. The storehouse held hardly two weeks' worth of flour and pork. Yet Gladwin had no intention of surrendering. Losing Fort Detroit would be more than a personal defeat, he was convinced; it would be a moral one as well.

A fundamental difference of opinion separated the commander of Fort Detroit from Pontiac's warriors.

This six-pound brass cannon, cast by William Bowen in 1755, was part of the artillery at Fort Niagara, a British stronghold northeast of Fort Detroit.

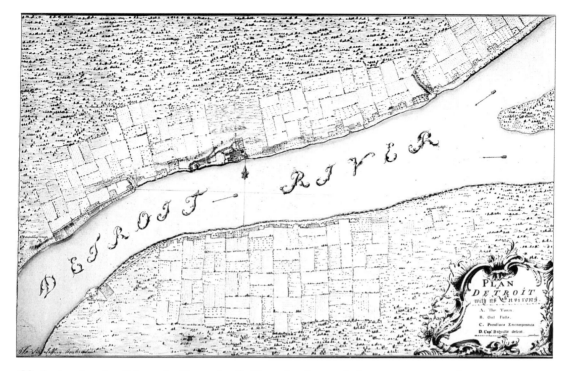

Gladwin simply did not believe the Indians had any right to the land of the Great Lakes region. The international laws in existence at that time, rules that governed empires and their colonies, did not grant rights to natives. Certain that his cause was just, Gladwin was determined to withstand the siege to the last man.

One night, while Gladwin was pacing the ramparts, an habitant rushed up to the major to inform him that Pontiac's allies, the Hurons, had recently captured two unsuspecting traders and their goods—17 barrels of rum and gunpowder. These were supplies the fort needed desperately.

Gladwin hit on a plan. Most likely, he thought, the Indians were now drinking the rum and celebrating. A small party of soldiers could steal out and man one of the schooners, slip upriver to the Huron village, and steal the gunpowder while the Indians continued their revels. Gladwin gave the orders immediately, and the schooner

This map of the area around Fort Detroit was drawn by a British engineer in the fall of 1763. The fort itself is designated by a small cluster of squares (center); Parent's Creek, the site of a major battle, appears toward the upper right, near where the river divides around the Isle-au-Cochon; Pontiac's camp is marked by a row of dots along the riverbank to the right of Parent's Creek.

soon pulled out from shore. Before the British troops could get halfway to their destination, however, the wind shifted and blocked their progress. Watching from the ramparts, a disappointed Gladwin signaled for the ship to return. The commander soon learned from a scout exactly what trauma the raiding party had been spared: more than 120 very sober Hurons had been waiting in ambush at the Huron village. Pontiac had anticipated Gladwin's plans and warned the Hurons to be ready for him.

The Ottawa war chief was not only treacherous but tenacious. No Indian before him had ever maintained a siege as prolonged as the assault on Fort Detroit. After two and a half months of attacks, Gladwin knew that if Pontiac's warriors stormed the fort's gates they would easily overpower his soldiers, and the last British garrison in the Great Lakes region would be in Indian hands. In order for the Indians to storm the fort, however, they would have to sacrifice many of their warriors, as the first wave of attackers would very likely be killed by defenders firing their rifles from the ramparts above. The Indians were not willing to accept such losses. Unlike European soldiers, who considered heavy casualties part and parcel of battle, the Indians believed that a successful assault was one in which no Indian widows were left grieving. Pontiac had clearly decided to use a much more deliberate—although less certain—tactic to capture the fort: starvation.

On June 21, the sloop *Michigan* sailed from Fort Niagara, carrying provisions and soldiers toward the garrison at Fort Detroit. Pontiac quickly dispatched a party of warriors to Lake Erie's Turkey Island, which the sloop had to pass on its way to the mouth of the Detroit River. There his men built European-style breastworks— temporary defensive walls—out of tree trunks and earth.

The wind died down just as the *Michigan* neared the

island. With the sloop's sails limp in the still air, the captain ordered his men to drop anchor. Night fell, and the Ottawas pushed their canoes into the water and paddled noiselessly toward the vessel. A British lookout spied them and informed the captain, who signaled his men to crawl up on deck and take their places on the gunwales. A few Indians had paddled their canoes under the *Michigan*'s stern to climb into the cabin windows. Suddenly the ship's cannon boomed, and muskets barked. Fourteen warriors were killed outright, and many more were wounded. The others retreated quickly to Turkey Island. No further attempt to storm the ship was made, and the schooner moved slowly out into Lake Erie to await more favorable winds.

The next day Pontiac dictated another letter to Campbell, warning Gladwin that Kinonchamek, the son of the great Ojibwa chief Minavavana, would soon arrive with 800 ferocious warriors. Pontiac suggested that the captain surrender the fort while he could still guarantee its inhabitants' safe passage. Gladwin instantly recognized the warning as a bluff. According to his own reports, Kinonchamek had recently chastised Pontiac for the long rebellion and threatened to make peace with the British. Again, Gladwin refused to discuss terms with Pontiac until Campbell and McDougall were released. In yet another letter, Pontiac responded that he liked the officers too well to return them to the fort and that "the kettle was on the fire [and] he would be obliged to boil them with the rest."

Soon the *Michigan*, still anchored in Lake Erie, found the winds favorable and began to sail up the Detroit River. On June 30, it finally came to anchor before Fort Detroit. Reinforcements and 150 barrels of provisions and ammunition were quickly rushed to safety inside the fort's walls.

This British achievement was a major setback for Pontiac. Desperate for the assistance once promised by the French, he called the heads of the local habitant families to a council in the longhouse of his village. According to Eckert, when all were seated, the leader appealed to them for support.

> My brothers, I am beginning to grow tired of seeing our lands encumbered by this carrion flesh [the English], and I hope you feel the same. I believe you are about ready to conspire with us to destroy them; still, it has seemed to me that you have been abetting them to our hurt. I have already told you, and I say it again, that when I began this war it was for your interest as well as ours. I knew what I was about.

Pontiac paused to lift a war belt above his head. "If you are French," he continued ferociously, "accept this war belt for yourselves, or your young men, and join us; if you are English we declare war upon you."

Pontiac's ultimatum divided the French settlers into two camps. Some left the council house immediately after hearing his speech; others accepted the war belt. One habitant, Zacharias Cicotte, declared, "I and my young men all accept the war belt which you offer us and are ready to follow you!"

While Pontiac was garnering French support, his white prisoners were seeking a solution to their own predicament. Campbell, McDougall, and Abraham Van Eps, a trader newly captured by the Ottawas, were being held in the back room of a house owned by an habitant friendly to Pontiac's cause. In the chill hours before dawn on July 2, while the Ottawas slept, McDougall proposed that the three of them attempt an escape. They could easily steal out of the house that morning, he argued, take cover in the forest, and race the few miles to Fort Detroit. Van Eps quickly took a liking to the plan, but Campbell was skeptical. Nearsighted, plump, and slow-moving, he knew

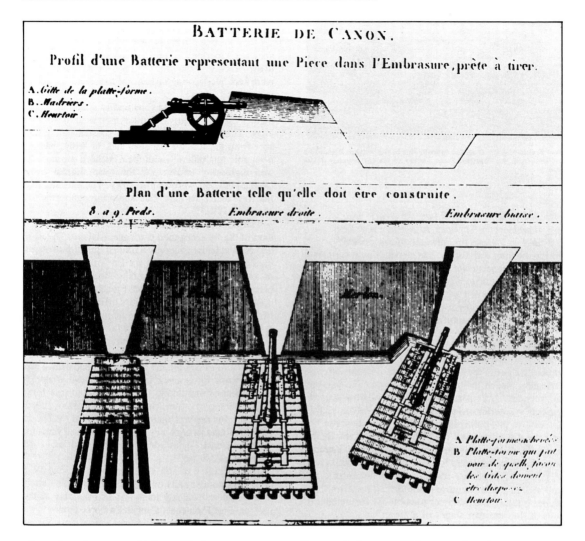

BATTERIE DE CANON.

Profil d'une Batterie representant une Piece dans l'Embrasure, prête à tirer.

A. Gîte de la platte-forme.
B. Madriers.
C. Heurtoir.

Plan d'une Batterie telle qu'elle doit être construite.

8 à 9 Pieds.   Embrasure droite.   Embrasure biaise.

A Platte-forme achevée.
B Platte-forme qui fait voir de quelle façon les lattes doivent être disposées.
C Heurtoir.

that the chances of his swift departure were slim and that he might hinder the progress of the others if he joined them. Giving McDougall and Van Eps his blessing, he elected to stay behind, hoping that his value as a hostage would continue to protect him.

McDougall and his companion soon loosened the shutter covering the room's only window, slipped over the sill, and ran into the woods. Awakened by the noise of the falling shutter, their Ottawa captors sounded the

This engraving shows a cross section and aerial view of a battery designed to defend a European fort. The cannons are supported by wooden platforms.

alarm, but not before the prisoners had made considerable headway. At daybreak, after a circuitous journey through the woods, McDougall and Van Eps were ushered joyously through the gates of Fort Detroit. Campbell's fate would not be so happy.

On July 4, Gladwin looked out over the northeast ramparts of Fort Detroit and saw an entrenchment that had been dug during the night by the Indians' new allies. Immediately he sent a detachment of soldiers to destroy it. The habitants and the Indians held their ground for as long as they could, but finally they were outflanked by a second detachment of British soldiers. As they fled for safety, two warriors were shot, and a soldier seized the corpse of one of the victims and scalped it.

Unfortunately for the British, this slain warrior was the nephew of Wasson, chief of the Saginaw Ojibwas. Upon hearing of his nephew's death, Wasson ran to Pontiac's camp and demanded that Campbell be handed over to him for revenge. "My brother," he told the Ottawa war chief, "I am fond of this carrion flesh which you guard. I wish some in my turn. Give it to me."

Reluctantly, Pontiac acquiesced. Wasson led the unfortunate captain away, and a group of Canadiens later reported that Wasson tomahawked and scalped his prisoner before tearing out his heart and eating it. Ultimately Campbell's body was thrown into the river and left to float down to the fort, where it was recovered and buried.

This bloody episode marked a turning point in the siege on Fort Detroit. Once they had learned of Campbell's gruesome end, the British became more determined than ever to fight. They knew now that their only chance of survival lay in defeating Pontiac's legions—and that if they lost, the fate that awaited them was horrible. Gladwin launched an offensive. Echoing Pontiac's challenge, he informed the Canadiens that they had to support the British cause or suffer the consequences. The settlers' provisions were taken forcibly and put into the common storehouse, and the young male habitants were inducted into the guard.

Next, Gladwin sent the sloop *Michigan* upstream to shell Pontiac's camp. The war chief guessed the reason behind the ship's movement and sent the women and children away from the village. Only the Indians' tipis and their contents were damaged in the attack.

On July 9, the Indians retaliated. They lashed together four bateaux, filled them with flaming tar and sticks, and floated them downstream. Pontiac hoped that the fiery raft would strike the schooners anchored off Fort Detroit and set them afire, but the British crews aboard the two ships managed to move their vessels out of its path.

On July 11, Pontiac tried the tactic again. This time he sent two flaming rafts, one after the other. If the schooners were able to avoid the first, he reasoned, they would find themselves colliding with the second. Yet this plan, too, was thwarted. The British fired their cannons at the Indians and so frightened them that they released the rafts too soon. The burning boats floated harmlessly past their targets.

Soon Pontiac found himself in a precarious position. In late July, the leader's Potawatomi and Huron allies told him they intended to abandon the siege unless a victory was soon achieved. Pontiac could not afford to lose the warriors of these powerful tribes. A council was called for July 25. Seventy Ojibwas from Michilimackinac and five Menominees from Wisconsin arrived to parley with the Great Lakes tribes. Pontiac described his strategy for the rebellion, reminding the Indians of the great victories already achieved. Always an inspired orator, he assuaged the other chiefs' doubts and persuaded them to persevere. Victory, he assured them, would soon be theirs.

Yet following this council, Pontiac's bad luck continued. A thick fog fell on the land on July 28, and under
its cover a convoy of 22 bateaux carrying 260 soldiers
slipped past the Indians to the beleaguered fort. These
reinforcements were commanded by Captain James Dalyell, an aristocratic and ambitious young officer. He was
a close friend of Amherst, and like the general he
underestimated the Indians' abilities in warfare. No
sooner had he arrived at Fort Detroit than he pressed
Gladwin to attack Pontiac's village by land.

Gladwin, now the veteran of a three-month siege,
pointed out that surprise would be impossible, that the
Indians far outnumbered the British, and that it would
be foolish to leave the fort's protection. Dalyell perse-
vered, insisting that the Indians would be routed by the
British and the siege would be broken. Gladwin, infected
by Dalyell's enthusiasm, eventually gave his consent to
the plan and even allowed the captain to lead the attack.

On July 31, at 2:30 in the morning, 247 British soldiers
left Fort Detroit and marched up the road toward
Pontiac's camp. About a mile and a half from the fort,
the detachment divided into smaller platoons and prepared to cross the narrow timber bridge over Parent's
Creek.

Pontiac, meanwhile, had evacuated his village and
carefully deployed a force of 400 Ottawa, Ojibwa, and
Huron warriors. Some 250 of the Indians had taken cover
along the road to the fort, where they had orders to attack
any retreating soldiers. The rest had concealed themselves
in the woods on either side of the creek. As the first
platoon reached the middle of the rickety wooden bridge,
Pontiac gave the order to attack.

The roar of gunfire, Indian war whoops, and the
screams of dying soldiers suddenly filled the night air.
The British had no idea where to aim their weapons in

the darkness. Several soldiers fell into the stream and the water ran red with their blood, giving the creek the name it is known by today: Bloody Run.

Captain Dalyell heard musket fire at the front of his detachment, rapidly followed by more behind him and on both left and right flanks. Realizing he had walked into a deadly trap, he sounded the retreat. As the troops withdrew they were attacked by the warriors concealed along the road. The brash captain was shot and killed, reportedly by Geyette, Pontiac's brother-in-law. By the time the survivors managed to return to the fort, six hours after they had left, they were dragging the bodies of 18 dead and 39 wounded. Other soldiers had been taken captive. It was, in one man's words, "a damn'd drubbing."

The "Pontiac Tree" looms over the spot where Pontiac and his warriors attacked Captain James Dalyell's forces on the morning of July 31, 1763. When it fell more than a century later, the huge whitewood tree still carried bullet holes from the conflict.

Pontiac and his men celebrated in the Ottawa tradition. They cut out Dalyell's heart and rubbed it against the British captives' faces. They killed many of their prisoners, then roasted and ate them—a ritual act that was said to grant the victors supernatural strength.

A Frenchman who attended the victory feast later said that Pontiac, after he had finished eating, asked him how he had liked the meal. "It was very good young beef was it not?" the war chief apparently said. "Come here, I will show you what you have eaten." The war chief then opened a sack at his knee and pulled out the head of an English soldier. Holding it aloft by the hair, Pontiac laughed. "Here," he said, "is the young beef."

7

BUSHY RUN AND
THE NIAGARA MASSACRE

This portrait of Tishcohan, a noted Delaware chief, was painted from life by Swedish artist Gustav Hesselius in 1735. After Pontiac and his followers captured several British strongholds along the Great Lakes, the Delawares began to attack the settlers of Pennsylvania, their former territory.

Pontiac's triumphs in the Great Lakes region left a deep impression on all who witnessed them, but his ambitions went much further. The war chief had told his followers he meant "to destroy the English and leave not one upon our lands." Inspired by this oratory, Indian tribes from lands as distant as the colonies of Pennsylvania, Maryland, and Virginia joined his warriors in spirit by attacking European settlers and soldiers in their own regions. The trader George Croghan estimated that the Indians killed or captured some 2,000 settlers and reduced thousands of others to poverty by burning their homes and property.

Like the tribes who fought alongside Pontiac, the Indians of the mid-Atlantic colonies had a long list of grievances to settle with their white neighbors. The Delawares had lost their fertile homeland in Pennsylvania territory in 1737, after a questionable real estate transaction with the sons of William Penn, the founder of Philadelphia. As a result of this agreement, known as the Walking Purchase, settlers had begun claiming Delaware lands; the powerful Iroquois had supported the settlers and forced the Delawares to migrate to the Susquehanna Valley. The Delawares never forgot this injustice, and when settlers began to move into the

83

Susquehanna Valley as well, the Indians began to wreak their vengeance.

In Virginia, 60 Shawnees under Chief Cornstalk ravaged the Kanawha River valley. At Muddy Creek, the war band was offered hospitality by two settler families. After sharing dinner with their hosts, the Indians killed them. Crossing the river to Greenbrier, where fifty people were gathered at Archibald Glendenin's house, the warriors were invited to partake of the three fat elk the Glendenins were roasting, and they joined in the general merrymaking. One lame old woman approached a warrior and asked if he could use his knowledge of medicinal herbs to heal her leg. "Yes," he responded, and tomahawked her. This was a signal for the other warriors to attack the startled settlers. All the men of the company were killed and the women taken hostage.

In the weeks that followed, similar incidents continued to shock and anger the colonial citizenry. Most attacks occurred in Pennsylvania, where the General Assembly was made up largely of Quakers—members of a religious sect that advocated the principles of nonviolence. The assembly forbade the militia to pursue and punish the Delaware war parties. Enraged by this attitude, some Pennsylvania settlers eventually decided to take matters into their own hands.

On December 14, 1763, 57 Pennsylvanians under Lazarus Stewart attacked a band of 20 peaceful Indians at Conestoga, killing many of them as they slept. The governor immediately called for the arrest of the vigilantes, but the Paxton Boys, as they became known, eluded the authorities long enough to raid the band a second time at Lancaster; by the time they were finished, all 20 of the Indians had been killed.

Quaker-dominated Philadelphia was horrified by these events. Benjamin Franklin, who later helped draft the

The Paxton Boys, a band of rangers from Paxton, Pennsylvania, attack peaceful Indians at Lancaster.

American Declaration of Independence, spoke for the city when he wrote, "the only crime of these poor wretches [the Conestoga Indians] seems to have been that they had a reddish-brown skin and black hair, and some people of that sort, it seems, had murdered some of our relations. Unhappy people! to have lived in such times and by such neighbors [as] . . . *Christian White savages.*"

The hatred and fear with which the frontier settlers responded to Indian aggressions was so strong that they marched on Philadelphia and threatened the General Assembly itself. Consequently, the Paxton Boys went unpunished.

The settlers' fear of the Indians was well founded, for throughout the summer of 1763, they had suffered violence at the hands of Pontiac's allies. Led by Chief Wolf, a band of Delawares and Mingos swept up the Monongahela River on May 27, 1763, and massacred an entire settlement at what is now West Newton, Pennsylvania. Captain Simeon Ecuyer, hearing of these killings, prudently ordered all the local settlers to retreat behind the walls of Fort Pitt for safety. The fort was soon besieged by Chief Wolf's war party. When it became obvious that Ecuyer would not surrender, the Indians split up. Some warriors continued the siege while others joined Shawnee and Seneca warriors who were attacking forts farther north.

The Senecas struck Fort Venango, 80 miles north of Fort Pitt, on June 16. They killed the 16 resident soldiers and forced the commanding officer, Lieutenant Francis Gordon, to write down the reasons for their rebellion— the scarcity of ammunition and the fear that the British would take all of their land. Then they murdered him as well.

The Senecas moved on to Fort LeBoeuf. They attacked with burning arrows while the garrison of 13 soldiers, commanded by Ensign George Price, took shelter in the sturdy blockhouse. At nightfall the soldiers escaped into the woods and made their way to Fort Pitt. The Senecas torched Fort LeBoeuf and burned it to the ground. Near Fort Presqu'Isle on Lake Erie they joined a combined force of 200 Ottawas, Hurons, and Ojibwas that Pontiac had dispatched from Detroit on June 2.

Advised by a renegade Canadien, this war party took up positions on two hills overlooking the fort. They threw up breastworks for a European-style defense and attacked at daybreak on June 20. Again and again their burning arrows ignited the blockhouse roof. The British soldiers soon exhausted their water supply extinguishing the flames. Ensign Christie, the commander of Fort Presqu'Isle, ordered a new well dug inside the blockhouse. For 24 hours the soldiers took turns manning the gunports and digging, while musket fire continued unabated.

Finally Christie agreed to parley with the Indians. The warriors told Christie that he and his men would be granted safe passage to Fort Pitt if he gave up Presqu'Isle. Christie was in an agony of doubt. His troops were exhausted and despairing, and there was little hope of reinforcements. He put it to his men and they agreed to surrender. However, as soon as they stepped outside the gates of the fort, they were captured and distributed among the tribes of the war party as spoils.

In less than a week the Senecas and Pontiac's Detroit detachment had taken the three forts that linked Forts Pitt and Niagara. The British were fast losing their foothold on the American frontier. The Delawares, Mingos, and Shawnees, now certain of victory, renewed their attack on Fort Pitt, the last garrison on the Pennsylvania border.

Captain Ecuyer, an unflappable Swiss mercenary, was not frightened by the horde of painted and howling

Fort Pitt (formerly Fort Duquesne) was besieged by a band of Delawares, Mingos, Shawnees, and Hurons in June 1763. A smallpox epidemic soon forced the Indians to abandon the campaign.

Indians at his gates. Fort Pitt was a well-built post, garrisoned with more than 300 soldiers. Ecuyer also believed that war justified extraordinary measures. On June 24, three Indians boldly approached the fort's gates and asked to parley with him. After informing him of the war band's victories at Venango, LeBoeuf, and Presqu'Isle, Kitehi, a Delaware chief, earnestly tried to persuade the officer to surrender.

"My brother," he said, "we who stand here are your friends and it is our earnest desire to save your lives. Already all around you there are a great many bad Indians who wish nothing more than to see you dead, but this is not the wish of Kitehi. I and my warriors will protect you from them if you leave at once, but you must do so quickly."

Captain Ecuyer refused. Perhaps, he suggested, Kitehi could persuade the other chiefs to make peace. As a peace offering, he gave Kitehi some warm wool blankets.

The Indians departed with their gifts but continued to make war. Within days, reports came back to Fort Pitt of a terrible illness sweeping through the Indian camp. As Ecuyer well knew, the blankets had been infected with smallpox bacilli. Within a few months the entire war band was dead, and the dreadful plague was ravaging the Detroit area. Ecuyer's tactic, an early form of biological warfare, was later outlawed by international treaty.

Reports of the loss of the Pennsylvania forts soon reached General Amherst in New York. Still stubbornly underestimating the extent of Pontiac's rebellion, he blamed the defeats on the forts' commanding officers. Amherst applauded Captain Ecuyer's terrible ploy with the smallpox-infected blankets and decided that the officers of the captured forts had simply not been intelligent enough to deceive their attackers. Amherst was certain that his good friend Captain Dalyell, whom he

General Jeffrey Amherst, whose indifference to Indian claims sparked Pontiac's rebellion, came to believe it was easier to kill Indians than to deal with them. He was gratified when an officer distributed smallpox-infested blankets to the Indians at Fort Pitt.

had only recently sent to Fort Detroit, would quell the uprising in a week or two. He was not yet aware of the extraordinary Indian victory at Bloody Run. The unfortunate Dalyell was already dead.

The Delawares, Shawnees, Mingos, and Hurons, feeling the effects of disease, abandoned the siege of Fort Pitt. At Edge Hill, 26 miles east of the fort, they crossed paths with a relief force of British soldiers commanded by Colonel Henry Bouquet. The war party quickly surrounded the troops and began picking them off one by one with bullets and arrows.

Bouquet ordered two of his companies to form a defensive circle. To the Indians it looked as if the British were retreating, and they left their cover in the forest and charged into the gap. Bouquet's ploy had succeeded; a second force quickly assembled behind the Indians and launched a counterattack. Suddenly compelled to fight on two fronts, the warriors broke and ran, but the wily Bouquet had prepared for that. Two more companies of soldiers began firing on the retreating warriors, killing many of them before they could regain the cover of the forest.

It was a victory for the British, but a costly one. Bouquet had lost 50 men, with 60 others wounded. Two Delaware chiefs had been killed, but overall the Indians' losses were not as high as those of the British. On the other hand, the Indians had suffered a setback that was more significant than numbers. They knew they had been deceived into launching a dangerous frontal attack, and this knowledge shamed and demoralized them.

Soon after the conflict at Edge Hill, which became known as the Battle of Bushy Run, a lull occurred in the war—a quiet and ominous suspension of hostilities at Fort Detroit and Fort Pitt. Such a standstill was unusual, Major Rogers informed Gladwin. It was unlike the Indians to just sit and wait. Usually they either attacked or abandoned the campaign. What neither man realized was that Pontiac had turned his attention to the portage at Niagara Falls, the most vulnerable spot along the supply route that stretched from Lake Erie to Lake Ontario and the St. Lawrence River.

Fort Niagara stood on the shore of the Niagara River where it flowed into Lake Ontario. Boats from Montreal, New York, and Albany loaded with provisions for the western posts passed by it, pushed up the river, and unloaded at a landing place, from which the supplies were carried by wagons up a tortuous nine-mile road to the top of Niagara Falls. Near the post there, called Fort Schlosser, the wagons were unloaded onto boats, which

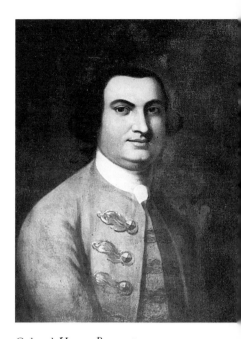

Colonel Henry Bouquet, a Swiss-born British officer who came to America in 1756, outmaneuvered a large party of Indian warriors at Edge Hill, 26 miles east of Fort Pitt, in July 1763.

then moved around Grand Island and through the rapids to Lake Erie. Ships coming the other way, from Detroit, anchored at the mouth of Buffalo Creek, close to the source of the Niagara River, where they were first unloaded and then filled with cargo from the eastern cities.

The first sign of trouble came when a band of Senecas was noticed by the guards escorting supply wagons up the road to the top of Niagara Falls. Some time later around 150 Ottawa and Ojibwa warriors were sighted in the environs of Fort Presqu'Isle, which was now deserted. Pontiac must have realized that the British would soon attempt to retake this important fort, and his warriors were waiting to stop them. In the meantime, the Ottawa war chief prepared to launch an offensive.

The *Michigan* arrived at Buffalo Creek on August 16, filled with soldiers wounded in the siege on Fort Detroit. The ship was quickly reloaded with provisions and a detachment of 17 soldiers. They set sail 10 days later, but a storm drove them aground. Miles from help, the crew and soldiers abandoned the ship, built a small camp, and prepared for an attack. Before daylight on the second morning, they were assaulted on two sides by Ottawas and Ojibwas. The Indians lay flat on the ground just 50 yards from the soldiers' defensive wall. Using a swivel gun, the British managed to drive them back. The warriors took up positions just beyond the range of the soldiers' gunfire, watching and waiting. Eventually, the soldiers were rescued by a detachment sent down from Fort Detroit on a second ship, the *Huron.*

On September 14, between 300 and 500 Senecas lay in ambush at a place called Devil's Hole, along the road that led from Fort Niagara to Fort Schlosser. The site's ominous name came from the dangerous whirlpool in the river below. A convoy of 25 horses and ox-drawn wagons,

This detail from an 18th-century map of British North America shows beavers building a dam "with wonderful dexterity" near Niagara Falls. The beaver was a mainstay of the European fur trade.

guarded by 30 soldiers, plodded slowly down the rough trail. A deep, stone chasm loomed on the convoy's left. On their right was thick forest.

Suddenly, a heavy volley of musket fire exploded from the trees. The mules broke their traces and stampeded, many of them plunging to their deaths on the rocks below. The wagon drivers became tangled in the reins; some were dragged over the edge of the precipice, others were trampled by the panicking mules. The soldiers, confused by the sudden chaos, could hardly tell where to aim their muskets.

In the midst of the terrible commotion Seneca warriors burst from their hiding places, tomahawks in hand, and killed the soldiers in hand-to-hand combat. Only two of the British survived—by hiding in the underbrush until all their comrades were scalped. The Indians departed, shaking the blood from their gruesome trophies.

Two companies of soldiers, meanwhile, were encamped near the landing at the bottom of the trail. Hearing the noise of the Indians' attack, some 80 of these men charged up the road to assist their comrades. Unfortunately for the British, the Senecas had anticipated their actions. Again they ambushed the soldiers, this time a mile below Devil's Hole. Seventy-two British soldiers were killed and eight were wounded—a loss greater than that of either Bushy Run or Bloody Run.

When news of this latest humiliating defeat reached Amherst, the general bristled with rage. Certain that Pontiac was the ringleader of the Indian attacks, he offered 100 pounds for the war chief's head—a great deal of money in those days. He also advised his officers from that moment on to treat the Indians of the Great Lakes "not as a generous enemy, but as the vilest race of beings that ever infested the earth, and whose riddance from it must be esteemed a meritorious act, for the good of mankind." He ordered his men to "take no prisoners, but put to death all that fall into your hands of the nations who have so unjustly and cruelly committed depredations."

The British and the Indians had each pledged not merely to defeat their enemies but to annihilate them. The terrible consequences of this dual promise would unfold in the devastating Indian wars of the coming century.

8

∇ ∇ ∇

NEITHER MONUMENT
NOR TOMBSTONE

Despite the Indian victory at Niagara, Pontiac knew that his warriors' commitment to the war was weakening. It was early September, and the cold winds that blew across the Great Lakes brought a warning: if the Indians expected to survive the winter, they would have to end the war in time for their autumn hunt.

The Ottawas were losing whole bands of warriors to smallpox. The disease was ravaging the Delawares, Shawnees, Ojibwas, Potawatomis, and Hurons as well. That fall, the discouraged Potawatomis and a large band of Hurons made a deal with Major Gladwin, surrendering their English prisoners for a captured Potawatomi chief. A group of Ottawas, meanwhile, sent a message to Gladwin declaring that their allegiance to Pontiac had ended.

As Pontiac realized after talking to a renegade Canadien, Fort Detroit was also threatened by the coming winter. Soon the lakes and rivers would freeze solid, and no ships would be able to get through. The *Huron* had managed to bring 185 barrels of provisions to the fort a few days earlier, but with these came news of the wreck of the *Michigan* and the massacre at Niagara Falls. There

A delegation of Great Lakes Indians meets with Bouquet (wearing hat, left) at a council fire in 1764. Many of Pontiac's followers had been ready to negotiate with the British since the fall of 1763.

would be no more reinforcements for the fort, and not enough food or gunpowder to last until spring.

The Indians' hatred for the British revived with the news that a band of Christianized Indians in Pennsylvania—men, women, and children—had been massacred by a group of drunken rangers. A Delaware band responded by attacking more than 50 settlers, killing many of them and taking the rest prisoner. But practical concerns outweighed the other tribes' appetite for all-out vengeance. If the fur trade was not restored, the Indians realized, their people would soon starve. Without European-made goods such as warm blankets, farm implements, and gunpowder, they would be unable to support themselves. The Delaware Prophet had been right: the Indians' dependence on white men's goods would bring about their downfall.

On October 1, a powerful Mississauga chief, Wabbicomigot, traveled from Canada to parley with Gladwin at Fort Detroit. Without consulting Pontiac, Wabbicomigot met with Gladwin three times to negotiate a peace. The next week, delegations from the Ojibwas and Ottawas met with the commander as well.

Hoping to stave off the inevitable, Pontiac called a general council on October 20, but even his magnificent oratory could do little to revive the rebellion. A messenger from the French commander at Fort de Chartres in the Louisiana Territory far to the south arrived in the Ottawa village, carrying letters from King Louis of France. These letters had already been shown to the Indian tribes and French settlers who lived along the Mississippi; they declared in no uncertain terms that the British and the French were now at peace.

The letter to Pontiac said, "What joy you will have in seeing the French and English smoke with the same pipe, and eating out of the same spoon and finally living

Mon Frere

La Parole que mon pere a envoyée pour faire la Paix je l'accepte, tous mes jeunes Gens ont enterrés leurs Castêtes, je pense que tu oublieras les mauvaises choses qui sont passées il y a quelque tems; de meme j'oublirai ce que tu peut m'avoir faire pour me penser que de bonne, moi, les Saulteurs, les Hurons, nous devons t'aller parler quand tu nous demandras, fais nous la Reponse, je t'envoye le Conseil afin que tu le voye, Si tu es bien comme moi, tu me feras reponse. Je te souhait le bon Jour.

a Monsieur
Mons.r Gladwin Major
Command.t au Detroit.

signé   **Pondiak**

On October 30, 1763, Pontiac sent this letter of capitulation, transcribed for him by a French sympathizer, to Major Henry Gladwin. Pontiac, responded Gladwin, would have to negotiate peace with Amherst himself.

like brethren." Finally the war chief realized that if the rebellion was to continue, it would have to go on without French provisions or ammunition. Much to Pontiac's dismay, the letter also stated that any enemy of the British was now an enemy of the French as well.

It must have been difficult for Pontiac to believe he had been so thoroughly abandoned by the people he had aided in the French and Indian War. A great French general had presented him with an officer's jacket and promised him aid. Disowned by the greater part of his own tribe, Pontiac found himself fighting a war that, from this point on, could only bring his people harm. Pontiac's rebellion was undermining the economy of the Ottawas; it was threatening the tribe with the enmity of both the British and the French.

To make matters worse, on the heels of the French messenger came the first snowfall. Pontiac took the only course of action available to him. On October 31, he asked the messenger to deliver a letter to Gladwin. The message read,

> My brother, the word which my father has sent me to make peace I have accepted; all my young men have buried their hatchets. I think you will forget the bad things which have taken place for time past. Likewise I shall forget what you may have done to me, in order to think of nothing but good. I, the Chippewas, the Hurons, we are ready to go speak with you when you ask us. Give us an answer. I am sending this resolution to you in order that you may see it. If you are as kind as I, you will make me a reply. I wish you a good day. Pontiac.

Gladwin, realizing that he finally had the advantage, refused to meet with Pontiac and sent word that only Amherst could negotiate peace. Then he forwarded the chief's letter to his superior, along with a note describing the situation at Fort Detroit:

> They have lost between 80 and 90 of their best warriors; but if your Excellency still intends to punish them further for their barbarities, it may be easily done without any expense to the Crown by permitting a free sale of rum, which will destroy them more effectually than fire and sword. But on the contrary, if you intend to accommodate matters in the spring, it may be necessary to send up Sir William Johnson. By that time the savages will be sufficiently reduced for want of powder. No advantages can be gained by prosecuting the war, owing to the difficulty of catching them; add to this the expense of such a war which, if continued, the entire ruin of our peltry trade must follow, and the loss of a prodigious consumption of our merchandises.

As usual, the pragmatic Gladwin had judged correctly. The cruel northern winter and the availability of rum would do more damage to the Indian cause in a few months than the British had done in a year.

In November, Pontiac decided to return with the French messenger to Illinois and seek advice from the

This French drawing shows an Illinois Indian smoking a calumet, or ceremonial pipe. Hoping to rally warriors for a final campaign against the British, Pontiac visited the Illinois tribes in the spring of 1764.

Delaware Prophet. Accompanied by his family and a few faithful followers, he left his home and spent the winter in two large Ottawa villages along the Maumee River. When spring arrived he contacted the Delaware, Shawnee, Miami, and Wabash tribes in Illinois, still hoping to strike a final victorious blow against the British.

The war chief arrived at Fort de Chartres in April, intending to persuade the French commander there to join him in a further campaign against the British. The French were uninterested, but the Indians of the region welcomed Pontiac as a respected and celebrated leader, and once again he was able to inspire these tribes to rally with him against the British. Soon, however, they added a condition to their support: only if the English invaded their lands would they attack.

Pontiac finally returned to his own village, only to discover that the Ottawas, influenced by a persuasive leader named Manitou, now supported the British. Even the renegade Canadiens had abandoned the cause. Pontiac must have realized that the chances of a successful campaign had become very slim.

General Thomas Gage, who had recently replaced Amherst as supreme commander of the British army in North America, soon received reports of Pontiac's attempts to revive hostilities, and unlike his predecessor, he took the war chief's actions seriously. "There is reason," he wrote, "to judge of Pontiac not only as a savage possessed of the most refined cunning and treachery natural to the Indians; but as a person of extraordinary abilities." Gage was apparently much impressed by the rumor that Pontiac kept "two secretaries, one to write for him, and the other to read the letters he receives," and that he managed them "so as to keep each of them ignorant of what is transacted by the other."

Gage decided to muster the colonial militia and urge them to employ the Indians' own fighting tactics—surprise, deception, and the use of ground cover. He authorized Sir William Johnson to promote division among the tribes by offering a reward for the heads of two Delaware chiefs who were still attacking British settlements. The Mohawks responded by attacking a dozen or more Delaware villages.

When Pontiac returned to Fort Detroit, he discovered that his allies, the Hurons and Senecas, wanted peace, and his few loyal Ottawas were wavering. In April 1765, he finally conceded that he could do no more.

Four months later, Sir William Johnson and George Croghan organized a peace conference outside the gates

The barricaded town of Detroit (pictured in 1794) overlooks a river crowded with British warships, Indian canoes, and small sailboats. In 1765, Pontiac signed a peace treaty near this spot.

of Fort Detroit. In the course of these negotiations, Pontiac told Croghan that the land belonged to the Indians and the French had paid them rent in the form of gunpowder, rum, and other goods. The British argued that the Indians had no legal rights to the land. They were not recognized as a nation by international law and therefore could not charge rent for use of the land. The British officers agreed to give the tribes presents in an effort to have good relations, but they refused to honor any land deeds as legal.

Without his warriors to back him, Pontiac could do nothing but concede, and a treaty was signed. With great dignity, he lighted his red calumet pipe and passed it around the great assembly. Each warrior, soldier, and diplomat inhaled a breath of the sacred smoke. The war was over.

Pontiac emerged from this council a changed man, hardened by disappointment. His intelligence and diplomatic skills had impressed the British, however, and they decided against punishing the fallen leader. In fact, their often-expressed admiration for the war chief caused disruption and jealousy in the Ottawa nation, and Pontiac soon became an outcast among his own people.

Accompanied only by a few followers and family members, Pontiac left his village and continued to hunt and trade in exile. The man who had once inspired 18 tribes from Lake Ontario to the Mississippi had lost his power and importance.

In his fifties now but still determined to spread his message, Pontiac visited the tribes of the Mississippi Valley to warn them that the British settlers would cut down their forests, hunt their game, and dirty their water. No one listened.

On April 20, 1769, Pontiac arrived in the village of Cahokia, where he planned to attend a council the following day. At this meeting, he intended to try once more to impress on his listeners their urgent need to block European settlement. A nephew of the Peoria chief Makatachinga accompanied him as he entered the trading post of Baynton, Wharton & Morgan in the center of town. As Pontiac left the store, the Peoria warrior suddenly pulled a war club from his belt and smashed the war chief's skull. He then pulled out his knife and plunged it into the great man's heart.

The reasons for this murder are unclear. Many Indians believed that the Peoria was a hired assassin, paid by the British. Others thought he was an agent of a Delaware chief that Pontiac had insulted the previous winter. Rumors abounded, and the British feared a new wave of Indian attacks. But Pontiac no longer had any ardent devotees but his old friend Minavavana, chief of the Ojibwas. Suspecting that Cahokia traders were behind Pontiac's murder, Minavavana killed one of their servants at the trading post a year later.

In an attempt to avoid blame for the murder, the British ordered Pontiac's body buried with great ceremony, but its final resting place went unrecorded. According to tradition, a Cahokia trader gave Pontiac's body to the French, who laid him to rest in the Catholic cemetery in St. Louis. "Neither mound nor tablet marked the burial-place of Pontiac," the historian Francis Parkman noted in 1851. "For a mausoleum, a city has risen above the forest hero; and the race whom he hated with such burning rancor trample with unceasing footsteps over his forgotten grave."

The Peorias were never punished for the murder of the Ottawa chief. Pontiac's widow, Kantuckeegun, was last heard of in 1807. His sons, Shegenaba and Otussa, survived in obscurity, although in the next century many Ottawa warriors claimed to be related to Pontiac.

In the late 1830s, some 60 years after Pontiac's death, Ottawa Indians camp on Mackinac Island, at the northern tip of Michigan's lower peninsula.

A drama about the conspiracy, *Ponteach,* was popular in the late 18th century, and a number of towns around the Great Lakes bear his name. Still, his substantial accomplishments might have been forgotten had it not been for the publication in 1851 of Francis Parkman's *The History of the Conspiracy of Pontiac,* which is still in print today.

Historian Howard Peckham sums up Pontiac's influence on the course of American history. The failure of his rebellion, Peckham wrote,

> exposed all the defects of British Indian policy, yet very few changes were inaugurated. . . . [Pontiac] appeared at a moment when the Indians desperately needed a champion who could think clearly, speak forcefully, and act decisively. By his program he gave full expression to the many injustices long suffered by his race. He typified the Indian attitude and empowered it with dignity, force, and direction. . . . He was a warrior of heroic proportions who set in motion the most formidable Indian resistance the English-speaking people had yet faced, or ever would face on this continent.

Pontiac proved that in the short run, at least, the Indians could defeat a better-organized and better-armed enemy, and this accomplishment instilled fear and hatred in white men's hearts. One result of his rebellion was the unfortunate government policy that called for the Indians' annihilation instead of their mere defeat. With Pontiac's downfall, "the only good Injun is a dead Injun" became the dictum of settlers across the continent, a population that gradually and relentlessly pushed Native Americans from their lands.

The Indians of the Great Lakes continued to support the British during the American War of Independence. As a result, the victorious colonists declared all land treaties negotiated by the British invalid. The way was cleared for the mass settlement of Indian lands along the frontiers of the newly constituted United States.

Waves of settlers migrating south and west were hindered only temporarily by the Indian leaders who followed in Pontiac's footsteps: the Mohawk Joseph Brant, the Miami Little Turtle, the Shawnee Tecumseh, the Seminole Osceola, the Sac Black Hawk, and the Oglala Sioux Crazy Horse. These are just a few of the leaders who were inspired by Pontiac to withstand white encroachment. They too were eventually defeated by the U.S. government, and their tribes confined to reservations.

History has shown that Pontiac's fears were well founded. The conquerors of North America did not stop until, 100 years later, they had ousted Native Americans from almost all of the lands that had once been theirs.

Cet Jcy vn
depúte du bourg de gannachiou
avé pous Alles imites au feu les
Missieurs de gandaouyoahga.
Jls tiennent que le ses portast
le dieu du feu, Jls l'inuoquent
le tenant en main en dansant
et chantant.

CHRONOLOGY

ca. 1725	Pontiac born near present-day Detroit, Michigan
1744	Pontiac's Ottawa warriors fight with French settlers against the British in King George's War
1755	Ottawas play key role in defending the French Fort Duquesne from British troops; some claim that Pontiac acquired his fierce reputation from this skirmish
1758	Pontiac remains loyal to the French despite British bribes
1760	General Amherst accepts the surrender of French forces in Canada; Captain Campbell takes possession of Fort Detroit
1763	The Treaty of Paris is signed, ending the Seven Years' War
Spring	Pontiac gathers 20,000 Indians at the Ecorse River for a council to plan an attack on all English forts on the western Great Lakes; Fort Detroit besieged; Fort Sandusky captured; attacks on the New York, Pennsylvania and Virginia frontier begin; Fort Pitt attacked; Forts Ouiatenon, Michilimackinac, Venango, Presqu'Isle, Le Bouef, St. Joseph captured by Indians
Summer	Battle of Bloody Run; Colonel Henry Bouquet defeats the Indians at Bushy Run; Devil's Hole Massacre
Fall	Pontiac ends the siege of Fort Detroit and leaves for Illinois to recruit more Indians and continue his resistance to English rule
1765	Pontiac signs peace treaty ending hostilities between the British and the Indians of the Great Lakes
1769	Pontiac murdered by Peoria warrior at Cahokia near present-day St. Louis, Missouri

FURTHER READING

Catlin, George. *North American Indians.* New York: Viking Penguin, 1989.

Dowd, Gregory Evans. *A Spirited Resistance.* Baltimore: Johns Hopkins University Press, 1992.

Eckert, Allan W. *The Conquerors.* Boston: Little, Brown, 1970.

Parkman, Francis. *The Conspiracy of Pontiac.* New York: AMS Press, 1902.

Peckham, Howard H. *Pontiac and the Indian Uprising.* New York: Russell & Russell, 1947.

Quaife, Milo Milton, ed. *The Siege of Detroit in 1763.* Chicago: Donnelley, 1958.

Tebbel, John, and Keith Jennison. *The American Indian Wars.* New York: Harper, 1960.

Utley, Robert M., and Wilcomb E. Washburn. *The Indian Wars.* New York: American Heritage, 1977.

INDEX

Amherst, Jeffrey, 14, 40, 43, 45, 47, 49, 57, 79, 88, 93, 96, 100

Bloody Run, Battle of, 79–81, 89, 93
Bouquet, Henry, 89–90
Brant, Joseph, 31, 105
Bushy Run, Battle of, 89–90, 93

Campbell, Donald, 16, 18, 44, 49, 50, 51, 52, 53, 54, 55, 59, 62, 63, 64, 74–77
Chippewa Indians, 13, 68, 86, 91, 98
Conestoga Indians, massacre of, 84–85
Cornstalk, 84
Croghan, George, 40, 41, 42, 48, 49, 83, 100, 101

Dalyell, James, 79–81, 88-89
Delaware Indians, 11, 12, 35, 38, 40, 41, 42, 47, 51, 63, 83, 85, 87, 89, 95, 96, 99, 102
Delaware Prophet, 51, 96, 99. See also Neolin
Detroit River, 19, 23, 24, 45, 51, 63, 65, 73, 74

Eckert, Allan W., 61, 75
Ecuyer, Simeon, 85, 86, 87 infects Indians with small-pox, 88

Fort de Chartres, 96, 99

Fort Detroit, 11, 13, 14, 15–21, 43, 44, 49, 50, 51, 52–53, 65, 66, 68, 88, 90, 91, 100, 101
siege of, 53–64, 71–81, 95–98
Fort Duquesne, 35, 36, 37, 39
Fort LeBoeuf, 36, 86, 88
Fort Miami, 45, 64
Fort Michilimackinac, 43, 45, 68
Fort Niagara, 42, 60, 64, 65, 73, 87
Fort Ouiatenon, 45, 64
Fort Pitt, 40, 85
siege of, 84–88, 89, 90
Fort Presqu'Isle, 36, 86, 88, 91
Fort St. Joseph, 66–68
Fort Sandusky, 66
Fort Venango, 86, 88
French and Indian War, 13, 35–45, 49, 97
Fur trade, 26, 27, 31, 49, 62, 96, 98

Gladwin, Henry, 16, 18, 19, 51, 52, 53–64, 71–79, 95, 96, 98

History of the Conspiracy of Pontiac, The (Parkman), 104
Huron Indians, 11, 17, 38, 49, 51, 63, 72, 78, 79, 86, 89, 95, 98, 100

Iroquois Confederacy, 26, 31, 41, 47, 83

Johnson, William, 31, 39, 40, 41, 47, 49, 98, 100

Kantuckeegun (wife), 103
King George's War, 30

McDougall, George, 54, 55, 59, 62, 74–77
Menominee Indians, 78
Miami Indians, 11, 99, 105
Mingo Indians, 37, 40, 85, 87, 89
Minavavana, 74, 102
Mohawk Indians, 51, 100, 105
Montcalm, Marquis de, 39–42, 97

Neolin, 12–13, 51. See also Delaware Prophet
Niagara massacre, 90–93, 95
Ninivois, 51, 62

Ojibwa Indians, 11, 17, 23, 26, 38, 39, 50, 51, 53, 62, 68, 74, 77, 78, 79, 95, 96, 102
Oneida Indians, 51
Ottawa Indians, 11, 12, 13, 15, 16, 17, 19, 23–30, 38, 39, 40, 41, 42, 49, 51, 59, 62, 63, 76, 79, 80, 86, 91, 96, 97, 100, 102
Otussa (son), 103

Parkman, Francis, 11, 12, 13, 17, 103, 104

Paxton Boys, 84–85
Peckham, Howard, 28, 104
Peoria Indians, 102, 103
Pontiac
  and Battle of Bloody Run,
    79–81, 89
  birth, 23
  Delaware Prophet, influ-
    enced by, 12–13, 99
  early life, 23–25
  ends uprising, 98, 100–1041
  family, 25, 103
  Fort Detroit, failure to
    capture, 15–21, 52–53
  Fort Detroit, siege of,

    53–64, 71–81, 95–98
  Fort Presqu'Isle,
    arranges attack on, 86–87
  legacy, 104–5
  masterminds uprising,
    11–14, 50–52
  murder, 102–3
  promissory notes, 63
  retires to Illinois, 98-
    100, 102
Potawatomi Indians, 11,
  17, 26, 38, 39, 50, 51, 53, 62,
  63, 66, 67, 78, 95

Rogers, Robert, 43–45, 90

Seneca Indians, 51, 86,
  87, 91, 92, 100
Shawnee Indians, 11, 38,
  40, 42, 47, 51, 63, 84, 86,
  87, 89, 95, 99, 105
Shegenaba (son), 103

Takee, 51, 62

Walking Purchase, 83
Washington, George, 32,
  36, 37, 39
Wasson, 62
Wolf, 85–87
Wyandot Indians, 11, 53,
  55, 62, 65, 66

PICTURE CREDITS

CELIA BLAND lives in Brooklyn, New York. Her poetry, reviews, and interviews have been published in a variety of magazines, and she is the author of *Harriet Beecher Stowe* and *Osceola*, both published by Chelsea House. Of mixed Cherokee lineage, she is particularly interested in writing about Native Americans.

W. DAVID BAIRD is the Howard A. White Professor of History at Pepperdine University in Malibu, California. He holds a Ph.D. from the University of Oklahoma and was formerly on the faculty of history at the University of Arkansas, Fayetteville, and Oklahoma State University. He has served as president of both the Western History Association, a professional organization, and Phi Alpha Theta, the international honor society for students of history. Dr. Baird is also the author of *The Quapaw Indians: A History of the Downstream People* and *Peter Pitchlynn: Chief of the Choctaws* and the editor of *A Creek Warrior of the Confederacy: The Autobiography of Chief G. W. Grayson*.